on track ...
Asia

every album, every song

Peter Braidis

sonicbondpublishing.com

Sonicbond Publishing Limited
www.sonicbondpublishing.co.uk
Email: info@sonicbondpublishing.co.uk

First Published in the United Kingdom 2021
First Published in the United States 2021

British Library Cataloguing in Publication Data:
A Catalogue record for this book is available from the British Library

ISBN 978-1-78952-099-6

Typeset in ITC Garamond & ITC Avant Garde
Printed and bound in England

Graphic design and typesetting: Full Moon Media

on track ...
Asia

every album, every song

Peter Braidis

sonicbondpublishing.com

Thanks and Dedications

I want to thank Stephen Lambe at Sonicbond Publishing for allowing me the opportunity to write a book about the musical career of Asia. It was a fun challenge that became much more daunting almost immediately after we agreed on me writing the book.

The week I began writing this book, the world crumbled in March 2020. Everything shut down due to the COVID-19 pandemic (which is still very prevalent here in the US in February 2021 as I write this) and the school I teach at shut down and eventually went to online teaching (which was and still is a serious struggle) and all college and professional sports halted. Seeing as I also work for a Major League Baseball team (the Philadelphia Phillies) that meant two jobs I couldn't do for quite some time.

To say the least, my writing this book as all this world strife was unfolding was tough, not to mention I had a hospital visit in April (and I am still far from ready to run a marathon) and a one-ton tree fell through our house during a brief, but violent storm in June. As a matter of fact, I was typing one of the last chapters in the book at the moment I heard the tree rip in half and hit the house which was a hideous, horrifying sound I cannot describe accurately. I couldn't even get the front door open because the tree was now our front porch!

However, the book is obviously complete for all to enjoy, and my love for this band and their music will hopefully come through in these words you read.

I profusely thank the love of my life, Michelle (the sweetest, most caring and giving person in the world), and the kids: Emerson and Luke (we are Emerson, Luke & Peter, so it was my destiny to do a book on a progressive rock band); our 18-year-old cat Krimpet, who is still spry and doesn't mind smacking me for no reason whenever I walk past her; our birds, and the mysterious squirrel that I feed every day outside our house who is waiting for me in a somewhat uncomfortable manner when I arrive home from work.

I must also give a shout-out to my co-workers and the kids at Rohrer Middle School. Somehow, we are back in school as a hybrid mix of online and in-person, and the kids are getting it done (as are we) under difficult circumstances. Wearing masks and wiping down desks may be the new normal, but here's to hoping that won't be the case for too much longer. To Doug, Stacey and the kids Meredith, Morgan, Christian, Quentin, Jon, Destin, Obaid, Tatiana, Collin, Kelton, Santino and Alyson: We somehow got this far and you will now forever be mentioned in a book! I thank Brian McRory for his help with the photos and his overall charming demeanor.

I must thank John Wetton, Geoff Downes, Steve Howe and Carl Palmer for creating this fantastic band and changing my musical life forever. I also thank John Payne for keeping Asia going with Geoff during some rough years that may not have produced great sales, but did produce some great music. And I also must dedicate this book to the late Neil Peart, drummer extraordinaire of Rush, who sadly passed away in early 2020 and was one of the biggest positive influences in my life with both his drumming and his words.

My mother really liked the music of Asia, and they were one of the few bands she used to not tell me to turn off when I was playing the music loudly in my room. Hopefully, she knows I wrote a book about the band. I miss her every day since she passed away, and like my other books, I dedicate this to her.

Peter Braidis
March, 2021

on track ...

Asia

Contents

Introduction

By 1981, progressive rock had become a dirty phrase. Most such acts, like Genesis, the Moody Blues, Jethro Tull, King Crimson and others, had shifted towards shorter, more compact songs, and steered away from the ten to twenty-minute epics of the 1970s.

When former Yes manager, Brian Lane, guided guitarist Steve Howe (who had played with Yes from 1970 to the band's breakup in early 1981) towards bassist/vocalist, John Wetton (ex-Family, King Crimson, Roxy Music, Uriah Heep, UK and Wishbone Ash), it was with the thought of forming a new band that could adapt to the new musical climate of the 1980s whilst still maintaining the musicality and sophistication of the 1970s. Wetton and Howe decided that a project together was worth pursuing, and under the guidance of legendary A&R man John Kalodner, it was time to form a proper band. Initially, the idea Lane had was for a lineup of Wetton, ex-Emerson, Lake & Palmer drummer Carl Palmer, and former Yes keyboard wizard, Rick Wakeman. They would combine with guitarist/vocalist Trevor Rabin, who had enjoyed success with the band, Rabbitt, in his homeland of South Africa, but left the country due to its Apartheid policy, relocating first to the UK and then the US. Wakeman later said, 'Because the record company (Geffen Records) were happy to sign us without hearing us play or even talk about the style of music we wanted to do, I refused to sign the contract on a matter of principle'. Thus, Lane moved on to a combo of Wetton and Howe. Wetton stated the importance of Kalodner in the Dave Gallant book *The Heat Goes On*:

Kalodner was key to this whole thing. He groomed me for the job, starting in 1976 when I played with Roxy Music at Santa Monica Civic Center. He was working for Atlantic then as head of A&R/West Coast. I'd just come off stage; I was just getting changed out of my stage jeans into my regular jeans and this voice behind me said, 'Would you have lunch with me tomorrow?'. I turned and saw John Kalodner standing in front of me. Then I saw the card he had in his hand... (it) said Atlantic Records. I said, "Why do you want to have lunch with me?" He said, 'Just courtesy. You're on Atlantic and I'm the Atlantic person'. When we sat down, he said, 'What are you doing? Get something together because you're worth a lot more than this. Playing backup to Bryan Ferry is not your destiny'. He gave me the best pep talk of all time. From then on, I would get calls every couple of days. He'd send me tapes to listen to. He kept grooming me towards this position. Eventually, in 1981, that was the time to do it. He'd moved to Geffen, and with this new-found position, he wanted to start up with a bang, and I was the guy he was going to do it with. That was it. I started writing songs that would become (the first Asia album). I could not believe how quickly it happened. From demo form, these songs went to Kalodner, and suddenly Brian Lane was there, Steve Howe was there, and everything fell into place so quickly.

Howe recalled in the same book:

Yes disbanded somewhere around January 1981. A few months went by,
and then the phone rang one day and Brian Lane said he'd been speaking
with John Wetton, who wasn't doing anything. We met in a small and poky
rehearsal room. and we spent a day in there, and John really blew me away
completely, playing the most incredible bass stuff. I thought, 'Well, forget
(Chris) Squire and the rest'. As it happened, the group would go in a
different direction, but I didn't know that at the time. We started looking at
some songs – maybe we spent a few days in there. They were the embryos
of songs, like 'Cutting It Fine', 'Without You' and 'Here Comes The Feeling.'
Basically, we were knocking around some songs and deciding whether we
could play together, who would be in the band and what kind of music we
would play.

**An attempt to recruit ex-Jeff Beck drummer Simon Phillips into the band
failed, but Simon was there for a bit. Phillips later said: 'I bailed because
I wasn't totally into the music'. Carl Palmer then entered the picture and
discussed how he came into the band in the Gallant book:**

I got a phone call asking me if I would like to come and play in a band that had
Steve Howe in it. Well, I'd known Steve for a long time, and I'd also known the
manager (Lane) for a long time. I came and played; there was John Wetton,
Steve Howe and myself – no keyboard player. I wasn't too happy with that
because I feel that with the amount of technology available today, not to have
a keyboard player is a bad idea. So I suggested we have a keyboard player, and
Steve Howe, having played with Geoff Downes in the last configuration of Yes,
suggested we try him. It seemed good to me, so the four of us played and we
decided to be a band after about a week, because it felt good.

**Around this time, it was a decision whether to add another musician and
become a quintet, which led to meetings with Trevor Rabin and ex-The
Move/Electric Light Orchestra/Wizzard member, Roy Wood, as well as former
Journey singer Robert Fleischmann. None would work out, but ironically
enough, Rabin would replace Howe in Yes in the near future, and he did do
some demo work with Asia before departing. Wetton told Gallant:**

When we first started, we wanted two singers. I was after that Everly Brothers
touch. But we tried so many people and we had about three or four songs,
most of which were my songs. I'd teach the guy to sing it and then at the
end of the day, we'd go to the pub and talk about what had happened that
afternoon. Everyone would say, 'Well, when you taught him the song, he didn't
sing it as well as you did.' The problem was that we were never really going to
find anybody.

Wetton elaborated on the subject of Rabin in the Gallant book:

Geoff and I knew all the time we didn't want any more people in the band. That was it. We had the four; it didn't need to be any more. We had the songwriting covered. We knew what the sound was going to be. But still, we got bombarded by people auditioning for the band. Trevor Rabin was one of the better ones. In fact, he was probably the best one.

A band name that was considered at the time was MI5 – after the branch of the British Secret Service – but with Rabin gone (he did actually rehearse with the band: 'Here Comes The Feeling', and 'Starry Eyes', which would later become 'Only Time Will Tell'), they ditched the idea of MI5. Wetton credited the name to Lane in an interview with *Kerrang!* magazine: 'We were sitting around the office with dictionaries, and Brian said, "Nobody has ever used the name Asia, have they?". We said, "Go away, Brian", and then the light bulbs went on! It's a good, strong name. And a name is very important. If we had been called The Architects, it would've been taken in a completely different way, even if the music was the same'.

Asia was signed to Geffen Records with huge expectations and began working on the debut album, *Asia,* with producer Mike Stone, who had helmed hugely successful albums by Queen, Journey and April Wine. In fact, Stone had just produced *Escape* for Journey in 1981, which topped the US charts and sold over nine million copies, with four smash US singles coming from it. Palmer talked at the time to MTV about getting Stone involved: 'We managed to get tied in with Geffen Records. David (Geffen) heard what we were trying to do. He loved the idea – the musical concept that we had – and he immediately said, "OK, let's do something". We decided to have an objective view within the group, i.e. a producer who was an English chap named Mike Stone'.

Kalodner was the one who brought Stone on board. In an interview with Dave Gallant, Kalodner stated: 'I originally asked Jimmy Iovine to produce the record, which he did not want to do. He said, "Why don't you use Mike Stone?"'.

Wetton was onboard with that decision: 'Journey, Kiss, Queen – you name it, Mike was doing it. Mike and I got on like a house on fire. We had exactly the same vision for the sound of the band. It was the harmony vocals on the chorus, the way that the vocal would be presented, in your face. Lots of keyboard layers and stuff. It was just exactly right'. A key ingredient that Wetton brought up was this: 'I figured that in order to survive in the 1980s, you have to stop being a band of the 1970s. You have to condense more and be more direct: cut the soloing. So you play for four minutes instead of the eight you used to play'.

What Mike Stone was able to do with the band was get the balance right from the combination of talent, and – as Wetton alluded to – bring in the accents on choruses and layer the instruments. The accent here was on the cohesive, collective sound, and not individual performances, which was more difficult to achieve than it sounds because these four musicians, legendary for their musicianship, were now being asked to rein that in. Stone did a masterful job in not only achieving that, but in creating an identifiable approach, which became the 'Asia sound'. You can clearly hear Stone's production of *Escape* – which was Journey's boldest sounding album to date – an accent on a group feel and one identifiable sound. The choruses and arrangements were worked out and carefully coordinated in an approach that was very close to what Asia would do.

Palmer mentioned: 'We have tried to create a sound collectively, rather than project as individuals. I was in a band where I could do nothing but project as an individual for eight or nine years, so I've had enough of that. I can go a different way now – and Asia is that for me'.

With a sterling cover and logo design by Roger Dean (of Yes and Uriah Heep fame), featuring a leviathan sea serpent rising out of the ocean, Asia also had an identifiable image to go with the sound, and the band members weren't even on the cover.

As for his involvement with Asia, Dean remembered it this way in an interview for *The Heat Goes On* book:

> Steve (Howe) did say he would like me to do the cover, but he felt that the rest of the band thought it made too much of a connection to Yes. They had other people do covers, including Hipgnosis, but they did not seem to get on with any of them. Late in the day, Steve said to me, 'We need a cover; we don't have one'. I said, "I have just the thing for you". I went in with a finished painting of the dragon and the sea and a logo for them. It went down very well. It was done independently of the band. But the logo was sufficiently different to Yes, and the dragon sufficiently different to Yes, and it was powerful in its own right.

And so, with an album of fantastic songs from start to finish, an amazing album cover illustration and logo designed by Roger Dean, perfect production from Mike Stone, and striking music videos directed by Godley & Crème that were tailor-made for MTV, Asia was ready to take on the music world. And the music world was ready for Asia.

Asia (1982)

Personnel:
John Wetton: bass, lead vocals
Steve Howe: guitars, backing vocals
Geoff Downes: keyboards, backing vocals
Carl Palmer: drums, percussion
Released: 18 March 1982
Recorded: Marcus Recording (London, UK) and Town House (London, UK) June-November 1981
Producer: Mike Stone
Engineer: Mike Stone
Cover Illustration: Roger Dean
Highest chart position: UK: 11, US: 1 (9 weeks), Canada: 1, Japan: 15, Germany: 6, Switzerland: 4

Asia was a musical and commercial phenomenon. The album got off to a quick start: in fact, quicker than anyone could've imagined. The record debuted in the top ten of the US album chart. Asia were initially trying to build up a following modestly – having booked the start of their first tour in colleges and theatres in the US, beginning in late April of 1982 – but this would soon prove to be impossible due to the explosion of the album. The first date was played at the Clarkson Walker Arena in Potsdam, New York, on 22 April 1982. During this early leg, they played venues such as the legendary Tower Theater in Philadelphia, PA, and the Stanley Theater in Pittsburgh, selling out halls that held between 2,500 and 5,000 people.

This is how the band wanted to build things – slowly. But album sales went through the roof, and the record quickly hit number 1 on the US album charts by May. Indeed, the album went to number 1 on three separate occasions, for a total of nine weeks. *Asia* went quadruple platinum in America (four million copies), and worldwide sales eclipsed ten million. Although Asia was a sensation in the US, they weren't quite as big in their native UK, though the album did well there, peaking at number 11 and charting for 38 weeks.

No wonder then that by June, despite having been playing theatres and colleges as recently as May, Asia were now filling 15,000-20,000 seat arenas every night and often returned to cities they had just played due to high ticket demand. Their stage design was impressive, and the band played impeccably, offering up the entire album as well as solo spotlights for Howe, Downes and Palmer. At the time, the band refused to play any material from their older bands, wanting Asia to stand on its own. However, this meant that they only had one album to choose from, even with the solo spotlights. Thus, two new songs were added – 'Midnight Sun' and 'The Smile Has Left Your Eyes' – both of which would be radically reworked for the *Alpha* album. Occasionally they also did the instrumental, 'The Man With The Golden Arm', from the 1955 film of the same name.

Asia also led to a Grammy nomination for Best New Artist Of The Year, though they would lose out to Australian band Men At Work. However, most critics despised the band Asia simply for existing, let alone for the actual music, and they hated the live performances as well. One doubts whether they even attended the gigs: and if they did, critics had poisoned darts out for Asia before a note was even played, and weren't going to change their minds. But none of that mattered to the fans, radio programmers, record store owners or MTV: all of whom were thankful that this 'supergroup' lived up to the billing, but were unaware that the band had delivered an album that would still sound fresh nearly 40 years later.

When I interviewed Steve Howe in 2001 as Yes were touring for the *Magnification* album, we discussed many things dealing with Asia. When it came to this album, I asked him if they possibly had any clue how big it was going to be, and he told me:

Well, we certainly hoped it would be. We were very ambitious at the time. We were also very hopeful. We were hedging all our bets on that record and we did it in completely the right spirit. Mike Stone kind of said to us near the end, 'You know I want to mix it'. And we kind of stated, "Well yeah, but we want to be there". And he told us, 'Well, give me a break. I've got to get in here and get it sorted out'. When we came back to it each day on the mixing days, he had already kicked its ass. (He had, for instance) brought those tympanis up on 'Only Time Will Tell'. All it took then was for me to say, 'Wait, you can't hear that bit', or 'That's a bit loud there', or "Can you bring that guitar break in just one beat earlier where I started?". These were tiny little things that the guitarist would notice more than anybody else, and there was wonderful continuity on that album. And what an album it was, with every single track standing on its own, even the one B-side. The album was that good.

'Heat Of The Moment' (Downes/Wetton)

The first song – on the first album – that was the first single and music video from the first supergroup of the 1980s, 'Heat Of The Moment' was to be the perfect way to usher in this new musical entity called Asia.

The song lets the listener know right off the bat that this was not going to be like the Yes, ELP or King Crimson of the 1970s. Steve Howe's opening, chiming guitar chords are unusually simple for the guitar virtuoso, and it works like a charm. The warmth of the sound is immediate, and as soon as the rest of the instrumentation joins in and John Wetton's vocal begins, listeners are hooked. The melodies and keyboard fills are perfectly placed and the chorus is instantly memorable. The verses build the emotion of the song, and the opening line – 'I never meant to be so bad to you' – was a shockingly honest and open way to start a lyric. The song was written by Wetton about his future wife Jill, although they would divorce after ten years.

While it seems like a simply written pop/rock song, it wasn't quite that easy.

The song was composed very late in the album sessions and was a combination of two separate ideas that Wetton and Downes had. There's also the intriguing middle-eight section with subtle keyboard fills and Howe's singular sliding guitar notes. Additionally, the song has unusual drumming throughout, particularly in the outro section.

And yet, it became a monster hit, soaring to number 4 on the US singles charts (and the same position in Canada), and number 1 on the US album rock charts for radio-play, for a total of six weeks straight. The single would stall at 46 in the UK. The music video was shot on film and was beautifully directed by the famed team of Godley & Crème. It used a series of sixteen grids, with the images constantly changing and telling the story, interspersed with shots of the band performing. The final shot shows a spinning globe landing on – where else? – the continent of Asia. The video would be played as many as four times a day on the then-nascent MTV.

When asked about the lyrical content of the song, Wetton stated on MTV:

It starts with an apology. You've never heard that in a rock song before, either. 'I never meant to be so bad to you, One thing I said that I would never do.' The whole song is just an apology. It's just saying, 'I fucked up. I hold my hand out and I got it wrong. I never meant it to be like that, and, so I'm sorry.' That's basically what 'Heat Of The Moment' is.

'Heat of the Moment' has become a rock classic. The song has been used in numerous TV shows and films, most notably *The 40-Year-Old Virgin* (2005) and *Good Boys* (2019). It has been used on an episode of *South Park*, with the character Cartman, passionately singing the tune in front of Congress, in the episode 'Kenny Dies'. The song has even been used for the popular *Guitar Hero* video game. 'Heat Of The Moment' was all the evidence anyone needed that the members of Asia did what they set out to do, which was to make a streamlined song with mass appeal, that could still showcase their individual skills as top-notch musicians and at the same time shed the excess of the bloated progressive rock of the past.

Wetton described the creation of this song in an interview on his website:

The original Wetton chorus was written in a country vein in 6/8. It was only when the Downes verse was introduced that we realized we could be going somewhere different. In a lot of ways, 'Heat Of The Moment' is a conundrum. The last consideration would be the first, heard by millions of people. Its chorus was 6/8 which became 4/4. The metal guitar-friendly intro was written on a piano. The natural key for anyone to play this song in would be D. We chose C#… the verse is in 10/8 time, and the middle eight (or bridge) begins with the most outrageous jazz chord ever invented on a keyboard but translated to guitar. The chorus chords are, uncharacteristically for me, or Geoff for that matter, all majors – a fact that delighted our A&R man John Kalodner, who was convinced (erroneously) that there had never been a hit in a minor key.

Then came the lyrics: not exactly the boy/girl stuff of our teens, but again what most people can identify with. Essentially, it is not so much boy-meets-girl, as boy-loses-girl and is tossing the whole scenario over and over in his mind, wondering how he could have been so stupid, but somehow justifying his case by quoting the chorus. The lyric metamorphoses into his life (real and imagined) towards the end, but always with the same result. I guess that really could be the true story of true love. It is in my case. We never do seem to get it quite right, do we?

One other thing we don't get right is the melody. Ask someone to hum the chorus and they will invariably get it wrong – they do every night when audience participation wades into our set. The vocal was recorded as a twelve voice block. There is NO lead vocal in the chorus. All the voices you hear are part of the harmony and all are mixed at the same level.

Downes offered his recollections of the song on his website:

My verse, John's chorus – that was it. That was written around John's piano. I think he had the original chorus, but it was a country song. We straightened that out into a 4/4, and it just seemed to knit together very well, as did 'Only Time Will Tell', except that I had the chorus for that. Steve didn't really want to play the guitar intro in the way that John and I had perceived it. He started to play a very broken-up version. We asked him just to power-chord it. He said, 'I don't do power chords'. In the end, he did it on a smaller guitar which had a bit more sustain – I think it was a mini-Gibson. It sounded very bright and powerful. We opted for that. We had to bribe him, I think! Steve was not enamoured with the song. John would probably tell you that as well. He didn't see it as being 'Asia'. And when Kalodner heard it, he said that it was the one we were going with (for the single).

'Only Time Will Tell' (Downes/Wetton)

The second track on *Asia* would also be the second single. 'Only Time Will Tell' is a very symphonic-sounding pop tune, based largely on Downes' insistent synthesizer flourishes. The main theme is carried by the lush keyboards, and Steve Howe adds beautifully-played accents on guitar, while Palmer plays tastefully and also gets to add timpani drum leading to the big choruses. Wetton delivers again on vocals in a sympathetic way that allows the song to connect emotionally without resorting to being saccharine or false.

The melodies and arrangements once again show how dedicated the band was to crafting songs and not just building epics like in the past. The scope of the song is evident right from the first note, the lyrics showing the pain of relationships and emotions, and some of the lines demonstrating excellent use of imagery. Here, the protagonist has been used and he is walking out not wanting to live a lie. He feels his partner will probably do just fine without him, but that only time will tell.

Listeners responded, sending the single to 17 in the US. In the UK it would reach number 54. The single edit chopped off a good amount of music but wasn't too offensive. As for the video, Godley & Creme came up with a weird one, as a female gymnast is leaping over a bunch of televisions on which we see the band. Though it's uncertain what that had to do with the song, it was constantly on MTV anyway.

Godley later stated that, 'We just felt it would look interesting; it's as simple as that. I don't think we were driven by it having any meaning initially. It was just the memories that came to mind as a device that might look rather interesting, and it felt like the music felt to a degree'.

In the rehearsal stage, 'Only Time Will Tell' was initially called 'Starry Eyes', at a time when Trevor Rabin came close to joining the band in 1981. It was one of two songs he rehearsed with the group. Indeed, Wetton had started to compose this song during his time with Wishbone Ash in late 1980, as well as several other songs that were prepared for Asia.

Like 'Heat Of The Moment', 'Only Time Will Tell' still receives heavy FM airplay. It was used in a *Family Guy* episode, a video game, and an episode of the popular TV crime/drama *Cold Case*. It's not clear if gymnasts around the world use the song to jump over televisions, but we can always hope someone attempts it at the next Olympics.

Downes recalled this about the composing of the song on his website:

It was just a melody that I had written with the chorus underneath it. Those two songs ('Heat Of The Moment' and 'Only Time Will Tell') were written in very similar ways. The intro came together when we started to arrange the song in rehearsals. We thought we would give the chorus a sort of pre-flavour as the intro. I took over the lead and played around the chorus chords with the fanfare. That was very much my signature tune.

Wetton commented on his website that:

(The song is) a lament regarding a lost romance: my first one. As lyrics in the second and third Asia record (*Alpha* and *Astra*) mellowed, the words on the first one were pretty nasty. I was castigated for that by (mainly) women – rightly so – it was a vitriolic lambaste, thinly disguised as a love poem. The fact was that it had a haunting melody and a killer chorus – augmented 5th on an A minor – in other words, the chord changes to F, but the bass remains on A. Invert it and you see the genius of Downes at work.

The lyrics to this and all Asia songs are universal. It is neither banal nor clever; it just IS. There is no obvious chorus like 'Heat Of The Moment', but it has the inevitable hooks.

'Sole Survivor' (Downes/Wetton)

This was more like it for progressive rock fans. 'Sole Survivor' packs an awful lot into its five-minute length. The opening is bombastic, heavy, and even somewhat gothic in tone, as it sets the listener up for a powerful ride. The song has serious drive, propelled by Palmer's thunderous drumming, but the verses are relatively open, accenting Wetton's vocals and bass-playing. Those vocals are incredibly strong, and Downes' organ, synthesizer and piano flourishes are all key to the song's progressive feel – each choice Downes makes has a deft touch.

The chorus is stirring and defiant, and Howe gets to add some wah-wah-heavy guitar lines coming out of each of those choruses. The middle-eight has a breakdown segment where only Downes is heard, playing a synth part that sounds like a creepy carnival. Palmer then hits the hi-hat, and Howe starts scaling up and down the guitar with more wah-wah, before a big drum fill leads back into the main musical theme, as Downes gives a brief synth solo leading into the final verse. The final section is a repeating chorus with Howe adding solos here and there, and Palmer building the tension with double-kick drumming and ride cymbal.

Wetton's vocal performance may be his best on the entire album. To hit that crazy note in the 'one time glory, back in their gaze' section, is impressive. John was finally leading a band, and he was going to make sure he left his imprint. In some ways, 'Sole Survivor' could apply to his whole rock and roll story.

'Sole Survivor' has long been a favourite of Asia fans. It has always remained in the live set, and for good reason. The song hit number 10 at US Album Rock, but failed to chart as the third single and only hit 91 in the UK. The single edit is an absolute butchering of the song, as nearly 90 seconds are shorn off. It's truly dreadful, but it is available to hear on the compilation album *The Very Best of Asia: Heat of the Moment (1982-1990)*, that Geffen/Universal issued in 2000. A sloppy music video was slapped together, utilizing the single-edit-butchering, over a dimly-shot film of the band playing at Wembley Arena. MTV didn't even accept it for broadcast.

It wouldn't be far-fetched to say 'Sole Survivor' is the best track on *Asia*, because it combines all the elements the four band members brought to the table and is a bold mix of the new sound with a few nods to the past. An Asia show would be diminished without it. When it came to describing this masterpiece on his website, Wetton said:

(It is) just a positive statement regarding our place in the state of the recording industry at the time. Indignant, if you will, and defiant. In other words, 'Sole Survivor' was a statement of the struggle – I'm not trying to sound pompous here – to get where we were going. The tense changes in the three verses of the song were not coincidental: the past, present and future were totally conscious. It was never easy. Our representative, on hearing the masters and seeing the artwork, told me, 'The logo is illegible, the cover is too dark, and frankly, I don't hear a single'. Two weeks later, it was the fastest-selling record in the history of the planet. Essentially it is a song of hope in the face of adversity.

'One Step Closer' (Howe/Wetton)

This wonderful song is the dark horse of the album. It is the song that gets mentioned the least, and hasn't been performed live as much as the others. Every massive album always seems to have a song like this. This song was the second one that Howe and Wetton wrote together during those first meetings and demo sessions before any other musicians got involved. It was mainly Howe's, but Wetton re-wrote some of the lyrics. Listening to the demo of this track that Howe recorded, you can hear that it was his song, aside from Wetton's outstanding chorus.

The song is a rich combination of melody, hooks and tricky arrangements, including a lot of start/stop movements, some of which don't have the same amount of bars. It's a neat way of composing – very much a Howe signature. Downes' keyboards provide pleasing colour, while Palmer and Wetton provide an excellent rhythmic counterpart. While the verses excel, and there are some nicely executed vocal parts, it's the phenomenal chorus that sticks with the listener. The harmonies are the real standout, but the song is also well-structured, including the bold keyboard fills in the snippets before the repeating song title lines, lined up with Palmer's snare rolls.

Howe's guitar solo on the outro is lyrical and adds a great deal to the overall feel, as he plays a lot of biting singular notes and throws in the classic lead lines so familiar from his time in Yes.

The song concludes with another clever start/stop segment, and everyone stops on a dime. The song was played live on the first tour in 1982 (along with the whole album) but would not appear again in concert until the 2006-2007 reunion shows.

'Time Again' (Downes/Howe/Palmer/Wetton)

Side one of the original vinyl concludes with one of the all-time classics in the Asia canon: 'Time Again.' This song combines elements of progressive rock, hard rock, and even some jazzy inflexions in the short spaces between the verses.

The track opens with a menacing riff in F minor that sounds foreboding. The second part of the opening includes a tricky run up the scale by Howe, Downes and Wetton in unison, while Palmer supplies accompaniment on the toms. Once the riff releases, Palmer strikes the gong, adding even more menace to the piece, and let's face it: any excuse to hit a gong is a good one. After another run-through of the riff, the song kicks into gear with a jaunt that seriously rocks. Wetton's vocals command the track, and the jazzy fills that come out of the chorus are clever and intricate. Howe really lets rip with his solo, and the song continues throughout with a head-full of steam. In concert, this song was always explosive – the band sometimes using it as an opener, to great effect.

The finale brings back the opening riff (complete with crashing gong) and concludes propulsively. 'Time Again' received enough airplay to reach 43 at Album Rock in the US and still sounds incredible after all these years. It was a group composition (hence the writing credits). There are no dated sounds, and this track remains a vibrant song in the catalogue.

'Wildest Dreams' (Downes/Wetton)

What a way to kick off the original side two of the album. 'Wildest Dreams' is yet another from the debut album that is an established fanbase favourite. Here we see the progressive side of the band in more pronounced form while still reining things in. It's not hard to imagine a song like this clocking in at anywhere from seven to ten minutes if it was from 1974. But it was 1982, and thus we have a fairly economic running time of just over five minutes.

'Wildest Dreams' begins with a thunderous intro that echoes the bombastic past (but in a good way) with all kinds of colour and musicality. The lyrics are anti-war and get right to the point from the opening stanza, which is accompanied only by Downes' piano at first. The vitriol from Wetton's pen and voice comes through loud and clear, and it builds from there with a series of striking images, some of which are violent: describing the fruitlessness, futility and waste of war. Further lines such as, 'We see the soldiers moving on to victory, And children trampled under marching feet, They fight for king and country, How many millions will they put to sleep?' show this was no mere pop tune.

After the second chorus, Howe's guitar solo in the mid-section is fast and furious, high up the neck, and one of the most intense of his career. This leads to the final set of verses and the most powerful of the choruses, giving way to an insanely speedy, dexterous drum solo by Palmer that is inspired by his love of Buddy Rich. Wetton's vocals on this track are nothing short of mesmerising, and the majority of the harmony vocals are by double-tracked by him. This song is truly a work to be proud of and had to have been a shocker to the casual fans who bought the record expecting a bunch of songs like 'Only Time Will Tell.' In fact, 'Wildest Dreams' garnered enough airplay to reach number 28 at US Album Rock.

There was a music video for the song (sort of) that did not have the band in it, instead using stock footage, mostly of war scenes. The band did not approve of it and MTV passed on it. This video was also included on the bonus DVD of the Collector's Edition of the compilation album, *The Definitive Collection*, which was tied into the reunion tour in 2006.

'Without You' (Howe/Wetton)

The very first song that Howe and Wetton wrote together, 'Without You' is a haunting, dark ballad, rich in complex arrangement, with stark melody and lyrics that cut through the soul. The song begins quietly, with Wetton lightly singing over keyboard accompaniment. Even after the other instruments kick in, the song remains dark and dramatic. There are a few instrumental breaks, where Downes and Howe play in tandem – the keyboards and guitars intertwined in some tricky interplay. The bridge is especially moving and tense and leads to Howe's first solo. Then it's Howe and Downes linked-up again, followed by a more mournful second solo from Howe. Once that solo concludes, some chilling acoustic guitar-picking leads to the final verses.

The cinematic, almost string-like keyboards from Downes accent the song perfectly during the verses. It's truly an expert way of playing with taste. The song comes to a sudden, quiet fade, played delicately and barely above a whisper.

'Without You' was only played on the first tour, being brought back in 2005 at the end of the John Payne years. It would, thankfully, reappear with the original lineup on the 2006-2007 reunion tour.

'Cutting it Fine' (Downes/Wetton)
Side two continues to move along in a progressive style with 'Cutting it Fine', an interesting song that starts as an upbeat rocker with driving bass and drums (the chorus really rocks hard), and then around the 3:20-mark, suddenly becomes a solo orchestral suite from Downes on eloquently-played piano, leading to an arsenal of keyboard sounds with a classical influence, as Palmer lays down some military-styled snare drum low in the mix.

Coming in at 5:35, once again, side two has a longer song. But even with the keyboard suite, it still doesn't get to six minutes, as the accent is on the song, not the showmanship. The keyboard suite segment on its own has been played live by Downes numerous times through the years, as part of his solo spotlight, and usually on piano. 'Cutting it Fine' (the full song) was played on the first tour, during the Greg Lake dates on the *Alpha* tour in late 1983, but not again until 2005. The song was, of course, retained for the reunion tour the following year.

'Here Comes The Feeling' (Howe/Wetton)
Asia concludes with its longest song, 'Here Comes The Feeling'. The origins of this particular song go back to the well-regarded French progressive rock act, Atoll. The band had asked Wetton to produce them in 1981, and he went to work on some tracks with them, as they had a potential deal with Polygram subsidiary, Polydor Records. The group had lost their lead vocalist, and Wetton offered to sing three tracks to help them get the demos done.

One of these songs was 'Here Comes The Feeling', and this demo (as well as the two others) was used as a bonus track on the remastered version of the Atoll album, *Puzzle Rock*, years later. The demo is very close to how it came out with Asia in some places and more of a mid-tempo rocker in other places where Asia changed the arrangements.

'Here Comes The Feeling' was another of the songs that Howe and Wetton worked on before Downes and Palmer had arrived, and it was Steve that changed the song, which is why he is credited as a co-writer with John. The finished version is wonderful, with melodic touches galore, especially in the verses, which ooze dramatics. Wetton's voice is sublime here as he carries the emotion of the lyrics, and the work of Downes and Palmer is exceptional throughout. What's especially great about this song is that it never follows the same pattern: the fills before the chorus get changed-up in different measures, which is creative and a bit tricky. These subtleties reveal themselves with repeated listens.

Downes has a keyboard solo towards the end of the track, then adding chorus colours that weren't there prior, again showing the creative arranging aspect. The song stops right on a dime with all four band members and is the perfect conclusion to a perfect album.

'Here Comes The Feeling' received enough airplay to become the 'sixth' hit from the album in the US, reaching number 40 at Album Rock. The track was also used as a B-side to the 'Sole Survivor' single, where it was hacked down from 5:35 to 3:30: an abomination much like the 'Sole Survivor' hatchet job had been. This version can be found on the same compilation mentioned earlier – *The Very Best of Asia: Heat of the Moment (1982-1990)* – if you need to hear it out of morbid curiosity.

'Here Comes The Feeling' was a great conclusion to an excellent album. Its precision, melodicism, professionalism and incredible consistency, made it a thoroughly enjoyable listen from start to finish.

Asia Rarities
'Ride Easy' (Howe/Wetton)

A song John Wetton was always very fond of, 'Ride Easy' was a B-side to the 'Heat Of The Moment' single and became a much sought-after item in the days of vinyl. In fact, this song never appeared on CD until the *Heat of the Moment (1982-1990)* compilation. The song didn't make it to the debut album more due to space constraints than anything to do with the song itself.

The track opens with Downes introducing a riff on a harpsichord-sounding keyboard. A powerful chord brings in the rest of the band, and Howe and Downes do some licks together before the down-beat verses begin. 'Ride Easy' is a moody and engrossing song. The track sports a great chorus, with Wetton delivering a classy vocal. The mid-section has Downes play an extended riff on harpsichord, with Howe tossing in some of his classic leads. Howe also has a quality solo that echoes his work with Yes on the outro of the song through the fade. The chorus has a memorable lyric: 'Ride easy my friends, This journey ends before it begins'.

As stated earlier, Wetton was proud of this song and later recounted to Dave Gallant:

Should've been on the album. Lovely, isn't it? It came from a previous era. I think it's beautiful. Remember, we're looking at '82 and there were all kinds of tricks going on then. They would hold tracks back so that they could put them on cassettes, B-sides of singles and stuff like that. It was all tricks to fool the bootleggers. That's why 'Ride Easy' didn't go on the album. Again, I wrote that on my own; I think it was in Miami actually, references in the lyrics go all around the world: 'Mexico to Paris…', if I remember rightly, that was my life at the time, round-about 1980, something like that. I didn't have a clue who I was. I didn't know what I was. I'd been on tour for about three years. I'd been around the world 85 times. That's where 'Ride Easy' came from. That was my identity at the time.

Fans would be thrilled when the song finally appeared in a setlist on the 2006-2007 reunion tour, and it went over extremely well, though it was sometimes played acoustically. 'Ride Easy' is the only other track that was completed from these sessions.

Alpha (1983)

Personnel:
John Wetton: bass, vocals
Steve Howe: guitars
Geoff Downes: keyboards
Carl Palmer: drums
Released: 8 August 1983
Recorded: Le Studio (Montreal, Canada) and Manta Sound (Toronto, Canada)
February-May 1983
Produced by: Mike Stone
Engineers: Mike Stone, Paul Northfield
Cover Illustration: Roger Dean
Highest chart position: UK: 5, US: 6, Canada: 10, Japan: 4, Germany: 11,
Switzerland: 18

When you sell ten million copies of your debut album, usually there's only one place to go from there, and that's down.

Alpha proved to be a very difficult record to make, and it would take its toll on the members of Asia. After the massive success of the debut album, Geffen Records had unrealistic expectations that the second album would equal, if not top, the debut. That was never going to happen of course, but when it comes to the record industry, rarely does common sense prevail.

Recording the album in the dead of winter – in Montreal and Toronto in Canada – didn't help. The team of Wetton and Downes (Wetton in particular, being the frontman) were under heavy pressure to come up with the goods again. However, their songwriting partnership only developed naturally during the sessions for *Asia*, as it wasn't some sort of pre-determined thing. Because the smash hits and other classics were largely (though not entirely) Wetton/Downes compositions, Geffen wanted John and Geoff to crank out hits again. Wetton even said there was no 'formula' for such a thing, and if there was, then he'd love to find someone who knew it. As it turned out, all but one of the ten songs on *Alpha* were Wetton/Downes compositions (the other was solely by Wetton). Howe was completely shut out – other than a song that was used as a B-side – as was Palmer, though he wasn't truly a writer as such. This created tension and division within the band and Wetton and Howe saw their relationship fall apart during the sessions. Steve felt his ideas weren't being listened to, while Wetton said they weren't good enough or appropriate enough commercially.

Whatever the case, it's obvious that *Alpha* had far less of a group feel than the debut. Mike Stone produced once again, and while he did achieve a beautiful, rich, textured and layered sound, it was with his mix where things went south. The keyboards and vocals became a wall of sound, and the guitars and drums got buried in the mix. Apparently, an early Stone mix was rejected, his second mix then accepted, though this seemed more by the label than the band itself.

The album had already fallen behind the initial release schedule. Stone was quoted as saying in *The Heat Goes On* book, 'The studio went down basically for three weeks. The album was supposed to be out – there was a deadline. There was nothing I could do. That took a while and of course, I took the blame. It's the way these things go – not that unusual. I was on my own there at the end and taking the blame for everything'.

As for what happened moving forward, Stone said, 'I was sending tapes out every single day. It was running behind because of computer problems. Then finally, there was a tape sent to John Kalodner, and I got called into New York for no reason at all. I said there's nothing wrong with them (the tapes). So I took a 15 ips (inches per second) spin on it and they were approved all of a sudden'. Stone also addressed the working-relationship deteriorating: 'The whole thing with Steve (Howe) was not comfortable at all. You know what it's like as a producer – you're in the middle of all this stuff. You've got to be diplomatic and you've got to explain to people why their songs aren't being used. Basically, they weren't commercial'.

The boredom of being cooped-up inside together during the cold Canadian winter, and the tension of making the album, spilt over into the tour. The oddball decision to start touring before the album was released was a mistake, as fans knew little of the new material.

Roger Dean again designed a gorgeous cover: this one in pastel colours, including green and blue, with a flying eagle, a pyramid with the now infamous 'eyes', a beautiful blue sky, a river, a dome and lots of foliage. It was a striking design. And with the album having a summer release, the warm colours really made sense.

Alpha got off to a great start with a smash single in 'Don't Cry'. The song also sported a video that was aired non-stop on MTV, and a Top 40 hit was achieved later that year with 'The Smile Has Left Your Eyes'. Three other tracks would chart at US radio, and the album went into the US Top Ten, peaking at number 6 (5 in the UK) and achieved platinum status. Sounds good, right?

Well, Geffen began moaning to Stone and the band about the perceived 'failure' of the record: a failure that sold over three million copies worldwide and a failure that most artists would've killed for. Alas, it was Wetton who took the blame, and this further soured relations with the label. The band was already feeling less than thrilled with each other, but they hit the road in late July anyway, starting the tour with a pair of dates in Cleveland, Ohio.

The first leg of the *Asian Invasion* tour mostly took in dates on the East Coast, as well as some Midwest dates and shows in Canada. The setlist nicely balanced songs from both albums and solo spotlights for Downes, Howe and Wetton still featured. Some dates were not well-attended, however, as bandwagon-jumpers for the first album hopped off, and the group were playing cities they'd played just a year earlier; thus, ticket-demand wasn't always there. Some arenas saw Asia playing to only 7,000-8,000 fans, where those totals had been 15,000-20,000 a year earlier.

The stage design was excellent once again, and fans saw a wonderful show, but behind the scenes, things were worsening. With attendance up and down, and the band not enjoying the way things were going, it wasn't looking good for the future. The first leg concluded very successfully with three straight sellouts of 12,000 a night in Pine Knob, Michigan, just outside of Detroit. The decision had been made, however, to cancel the second leg of the tour, which was headed for the Midwest, South and West coasts of the US in the fall. Wetton took a two-week vacation in France. He claims he was then fired; others say he quit. But one thing was certain: Wetton was gone, and Asia had lost their frontman and their voice.

Greg Lake (solo artist and ex-King Crimson and ELP) came in to replace Wetton. On paper, it made sense. Greg was an awesome bassist/vocalist, who'd played a decade with Palmer in ELP, and had always had a knack for pop/rock songs in his solo career and even in ELP. The tour resumed on 6 December 1983 at the sold-out Nippon Budokan Hall in Tokyo, Japan. The gig was billed as *Asia in Asia* and would be viewed by over 20 million people worldwide. After the Japanese shows, the band broke for the Christmas holidays, and Greg Lake departed.

Asia was a mess. Management had pushed Wetton out, and the band, the fans and the media, were baffled. Wetton would return in early 1984, but then Howe departed. Little did anyone know that *Alpha* would be the last studio album by the original lineup until 2008.

In our interview from 2001, Howe offered me his thoughts as to what went wrong with the band and *Alpha*:

Well, you know, Asia thought it had established something on the first album, and what it thought it could do on the second album was – dare I say the word – capitalise, but capitalise and also commercialise the direction, and therefore, why I'm saying this is if it's clearer that the guitar and keyboard work were a modernised sound, that's what happened.

This was part of the Asia goal, to have this sort of '80s sound. We did it so much better on the first record, where we poked things out and we had more colour. We had more colour in the structures, because here and there, lo and behold, there were Steve Howe guitar chord sequences and you know, the second album… bless them (John and Geoff), because they really took the bull by the horns and started writing endless amounts of songs… but we could've done with a few less of them and a few more songs that didn't rest on the keyboard direction, because the original Asia record was about the four members and a universal sound. We're talking about the swapping of parts into a more homogenised sound, as opposed to featuring sounds where you'd go, 'Hey, that's Steve, hey that's Geoff and listen to Carl's drumming, it's all coming through'. I know Carl was unhappy with some of his drum sounds on the album. The balance, you know, it wasn't a band vision record. The first album was a band vision and producer vision. We managed to collaborate, and on the second album, the collaboration was more about the difficulties of getting things approved, so that was a bit tough. I think what we recorded was fair, but what we mixed never really settled in any areas to be the right sort of balance. I would've liked it to be mixed like the first album, but I also don't think we had the material.

'Don't Cry' (Downes/Wetton)

Like that of the debut album, the opening song on *Alpha* would be the first single and video and was also written towards the end of the sessions, as 'Heat of the Moment' had been with *Asia*. 'Don't Cry' opens up the first side which is listed as the *Alpha* side (the *Beta* was side two).

'Don't Cry' is an infectious pop/rock song with an irresistible hook and melody and another outstanding vocal from Wetton. The song is on the soft side, with lush keyboards and a production and mix that offer warmth, with a heavy accent on the vocal and keyboard sounds. There are not many lyrics (only two sets of verses), while the chorus repeats throughout, especially after the brief instrumental break. There are no guitar or keyboard solos, so this song really goes for a pop style and does so, well.

Although many of the songs on *Alpha* tend to bury Howe and Palmer in the mix, this one allows both players to be heard, with the opening and the mid-section seeing Howe adding appropriate 'crying' guitar and Palmer getting in some licks on drums. The song flies by and it was a great summer single – another smash reaching number 10 on the US singles charts, soaring to number one at Album Rock, and charting a total of fourteen weeks. 'Don't Cry' was also the band's lone Top 40 single in the UK, reaching 33.

The MTV video allowed the guys to have some fun and was directed by Brian Grant, who did some amazing videos for acts like The Fixx, Peter Gabriel ('Shock The Monkey'), Queen, Duran Duran, XTC and more. The video cost $100,000 to make, which was becoming typical for the times, and was shot on film at Twickenham Film Studios. It was a *Raiders of the Lost Ark*-inspired clip, looked great on film, and was constantly played on MTV as much as four times a day.

Live, the song never really came off that well. It was a highly-produced track and recreating that 'wall of sound' live was tough. In subsequent years, they have played it acoustically, tried it with a bit of a harder edge, and stripped it down to just piano and voice. Greg Lake and John Payne both did a fairly good job with it live. But vocally, this song is totally Wetton and is ample evidence of what an excellent vocalist he was, and that you can't just throw someone in there and make a song like this sound right (as they have in recent years with Billy Sherwood and Ron Thal).

'The Smile Has Left Your Eyes' (Wetton)

We have now arrived at my favourite song written by anyone. 'The Smile Has Left Your Eyes' has such a frail beauty to it, words cannot do it justice, but I shall try.

It was solely written by Wetton, though it was actually about Downes. Geoff had endured a painful breakup about a year or so before, and Wetton remembered it. He was quoted as saying to *songfacts.com*, 'I identified so strongly with that, I went home and wrote the song in five minutes. Boom! Sat right down at the piano and there it was. If anything's straight from the heart, that song is'.

After a few lush keyboard intro chords from Geoff, he plays a pretty-sounding part as John introduces the lyrics, and it becomes emotional and moving, right from the opening line. Once the drums, guitars and bass come in, the song's beauty escalates, but the lyric continues to show the pain. Although it tells a tale we all know – of being left for another – it shows the devastation such a situation can cause and says it all in the lines, 'It's over now, It's not my fault, See how this feels for you'.

The verses have a sweeping, understated quality that allows each member their own unique contribution. Palmer deftly uses his toms to accent the lines in the song, and Howe plays subtle but effective guitar fills throughout in his classic Yes style – also adding a bit of that Chet Atkins influence in his picking technique – while Downes sweeps in his vibrant colours on the keyboards, and Wetton sings wonderfully and impassioned. Things shift to a minor chord for the moving bridge, where the pain is exacerbated with the lyric, 'I never thought I'd see you standing there with him, So don't come crawlin' back to me'. While this is going on, there are some stunning Beach Boys-style backing vocals (Wetton was a massive Beach Boys fan, so I wouldn't doubt this was an influence) and some perfectly placed arpeggios from Howe on guitar.

The main theme with Downes keyboards and Wetton's voice takes us back to the beginning, with the same opening line of, 'I saw you standing hand in hand'. This time, the drums and guitars come in with more force, as the hurt, anger and betrayal increase with that musical 'wall of sound' approach, used to good effect in this instance. After another chorus, you almost feel as though it's going to end right there, but yet one more chorus hits harder, with forceful power chords from all, and Wetton's voice begins to crack, giving in to the emotion until the final two chords strike.

A tender piano plays as John sings the song's title quietly at the end. And we get all of this in only three minutes and thirteen seconds. If you don't feel something listening to this song, I weep for you, my friend.

The 1983 demo version was largely the whole song on piano and vocals through the first half, followed by the dramatic full-band second part, which essentially repeated things, but in grandiose style. It's pretty much the way you hear it on *Live in Moscow* from 1991. It's a fascinating listen, comparing it with the version that ended up on *Alpha*.

The music video was again directed by Brian Grant and was made to look like a classic French cinematic drama, complete with subtitles. Stunningly shot on film, in widescreen, it intersperses clips of the band playing the track in the studio, with three main characters on screen: Danielle (played by

Natasha King) and her parents Jacques (Terry Grant) and Chantale (Vivienne Chandler). Young Danielle is witnessing the disintegration of her parents' marriage, and her mother has a new man. Jacques isn't handling it well and he's missing his daughter. Danielle can't handle it all and goes missing. Her parents unite to find her, in a frantic search that seems to end tragically as they see her doll floating in the river while they stand upon a bridge. The parents cry in unison and the picture freezes. But as the song ends, who is looking at Wetton in the studio doorway, but Danielle, with a smile that has not left her eyes. This is a tremendous video that has stood the test of time (just look at the thousands and thousands of views and comments on YouTube).

'The Smile Has Left Your Eyes' was issued as a single, with Wetton gone from the band in September and the second leg of the US tour scrapped. It was still a Top 40 single in the US, reaching 34, and hit 25 at Album Rock. In the UK it crawled to 81.

Live versions varied over the years, from a sparse piano and vocal version (Greg Lake did it this way for the *Asia in Asia* concert) to an acoustic version (this can be seen and heard on the 2007 CD and DVD, *Fantasia Live in Tokyo*, where it has a decidedly country/rock feel with sparse instrumentation), and the powerful two-part version which can be heard at its absolute best live on the 2017 release, *Symfonia-Live in Bulgaria 2013*, where Wetton sings his heart out.

'Never In A Million Years' (Downes/Wetton)
The next track on the album is a decent song that is pretty to listen to, especially at chorus time but is largely dominated by the lush, symphonic keyboards of Downes and Wetton's vocals. To be sure, this is a pleasant, well-constructed song, and Howe has a touch of wah-wah guitar during the intro, which is repeated later on.

However, it doesn't stand out all that much and leans a little too close to a softer sound that fans of the first album were probably not thrilled with. The lyrics are a bit on the weak side as well. Howe's guitars are there somewhere, but really only on the intro and its later repeat. This is a nice enough song, and boy does Wetton sound great, but it's just too light and seems to settle for that.

Howe told me in our interview from 2001 that this song was supposed to be quite different:

> On *Alpha*, I fought like mad to be able to hear myself, occasionally, or not to be edited. There was quite an interesting beginning, I thought, on 'Never In A Million Years', where there was this clangy and weirdo guitar intro, and then the rest of the band would join in: and before I knew it, it was hacked off. This wasn't so much the band, I've got to say – it wasn't primarily the band or particularly Mike Stone, but we were being affected by the record company and the person there. It was very sad to feel your work isn't fully being appreciated.

'My Own Time (I'll Do What I Want)' (Downes/Wetton)

The band coalesce well on this spirited song with an instantly likeable hook. It has a thunderous opening – like a vintage Yes song – and then Howe does some nifty acoustic guitar-picking for the first verse. Wetton is so well-suited to songs of this nature; it's no wonder Asia worked so well.

Once again, we seem to have someone scorned, as Wetton begins the tale of the protagonist, who has been dumped but is now starting to realize he's not only going to rebound, he's going to be better off. There's a great line at the end of the second verse where Wetton proclaims, 'Something you didn't learn, Faith in myself, Gives me the strength to carry on'. One could use this in any facet of life, not just relationships, but it's a great line that leads to a chorus with undeniable spirit.

The chorus chords are warm, as is the overall feel, even though the album was recorded in the dead of Canada's frigid winter! The last-minute of the song lets Howe wail with some bite and grit on lead guitar, Downes then sending the song out on the fade with a glorious trumpet-like keyboard part. Palmer adds double kick-drum fills and ride cymbal. Though this great track did not get played live for many years, it surfaced in latter-day setlists, and strong versions appear on the live releases, *Symfonia* and *Spirit of the Night*.

The demo version is very similar, but only the melody is sung on the verses, with the chorus intact and most of the instrumentation the same.

'The Heat Goes On' (Downes/Wetton)

One of the most popular songs in the Asia canon, 'The Heat Goes On' is a surprising rocker that has been a part of virtually every concert the band has performed since 1983. The song opens with a piano fill that builds into a full-band assault – aside from a short, melodic bridge – and pretty much rocks from there.

Howe plays a pretty prominent role here, with some scorching leads and even some pull-offs. The chorus is one of the strongest on the album. The song really sets the listener up for a blistering, somewhat lengthy, Downes organ solo that has always been fun live. He plays the intro again at the end, this time on organ, the full band then quickly building to the stop. At just under five minutes, this is the second-longest song on *Alpha*. It's one of the genuinely few aggressive and progressive moments on the album and had many fans griping that they wanted more material like this and less of the symphonic pop material.

In concert, this song usually featured Palmer's drum solo, something he had done before on songs such as 'Wildest Dreams' and 'Here Comes The Feeling.' To the present day, the drum solo has almost always come at the conclusion of 'The Heat Goes On.' In the late summer of 1983, when *Alpha* came out, 'The Heat Goes On' received a lot of FM airplay in the US, sending it all the way to number five at Album Rock. Greg Lake did a fine job on this live (a live clip from the *Asia in Asia* concert was used as a video for a short time on MTV), as did John Payne in the later years.

'Eye To Eye' (Downes/Wetton)

Here is a little-discussed song from the classic Asia years. It's a quality one that opens up side two (or the *Beta* side as it was called). The song flies by quickly, at barely over three minutes in length. It certainly seems to have been a bit chopped up because the fade is abrupt and disappointing – especially as both Howe and Downes are trading solos at that point.

'Eye To Eye' has a quirky, new wave feel about it, especially in the pre-chorus parts which have a snaky little keyboard line that wouldn't be out of place on a song from Duran Duran or Ultravox. Howe does some arpeggio lines on the chorus, and Wetton sings high up the register at some points. Once more, we revisit the theme of a failed relationship, Wetton singing a great couplet: 'Can you give me reasons why I made this sacrifice? When you thought you walked on water, You were skating on thin ice'. The chorus, which repeats, ''Cause we don't see eye to eye', could be interpreted as Wetton singing about Howe.

This particular song was played live only on the *Asian Invasion* tour supporting *Alpha*. It came across much better live, especially as we got to hear both Howe and Downes extend themselves with their solos. The band also played this tune for the *Asia in Asia* concert with Greg Lake. Steve really plays exceptional lead on that version, though Greg seems a little uncomfortable delivering it.

'The Last To Know' (Downes/Wetton)

More musical drama for the scorned, 'The Last to Know' is another heartbreaking tale of woe, and is beautifully detailed. Wetton sings passionately, and the chorus soars with Downes' keyboards and Howe's lead lines. Interestingly enough, the chorus sounds upbeat and hopeful, while the verses concentrate more on the anguish. This is a song that really showcases the melodic skill Wetton and Downes brought to the band.

The mid-section has a classically-inspired keyboard part, with staccato guitar lines and Palmer's tight accents. It's a dramatic change, but it builds to more choruses until the conclusion. 'The Last to Know' was played live on select dates of the 1983 tour but was dropped afterwards. The demo version is similar to the final arrangement but lacks bass and guitars, with Wetton singing the melody only in the verses before singing the actual chorus.

'True Colours' (Downes/Wetton)

Although this is a pretty good song (especially the bridge), this might've been better dropped from the album and used as one of the (mostly superior) B-sides that were left off. By this point in the album, softer-sounding songs such as this one were getting a little tiresome. The lushness is on display yet again, and it becomes obvious that *Alpha* just wasn't going to be as inventive or exciting as the debut.

The chorus springs to life a little bit, but overall the song feels like it could've used more development in the verses. The bridge is really strong, though, with

Wetton climbing the heights of his vocal range. 'True Colours' received enough airplay in the US to reach number 20 on the Album Rock charts. The song was performed live on some dates in 1983 and also surfaced in the obscure shows that Wetton and Palmer played in Europe in 1989 that led to the band reforming for real in 1990.

The demo version lacks lyrics in the verses and bridge, but the outline of the song is there. Palmer's drums sound stronger on the demos and so much on this song that it's a shame how they were mixed on the album itself.

'Midnight Sun' (Downes/Wetton)

This song actually debuted on the 1982 tour in a very different form, though some elements were retained. It's certainly one of the *Alpha* tracks which echoes the classic sound established on the debut.

It's easy to picture Roger Dean's album cover as we hear this song. Unfortunately, Wetton's vocals are drenched in too much reverb, Howe's guitars are mixed too low, and Palmer's drums are largely buried in the sound. But the keyboards and vocals carry the song to a land of beauty: this land of the midnight sun (is it Alaska? Norway? Iceland? My geography lessons tell me it could be any of these).

At least Howe gets to unleash a tension-filled guitar solo, but it's the only time he really stands out in the song. An interesting fact is that the verses are in the strange time signature of 7/4. That's hardly common and definitely of a progressive rock mindset. The track definitely could've been lengthened beyond the short running time of 3:48. It still feels quite grand, though, with a big panoramic sound.

The 1983 demo had no lead guitars, but the structure was there. As was the lyric, which makes sense, as the song was played on the first tour in 1982, albeit in a much different fashion, with everyone on electric percussion at one point.

'Open Your Eyes' (Downes/Wetton)

Here is one sure to please the progressive rock fans complaining that Asia was too homogenised or commercial. Clocking in at nearly six and a half minutes, 'Open Your Eyes' is progressive indeed. The song begins with Downes using chilling choral keyboards and vocoder (a voice synthesizer). The lyrics seem to be telling a woman not to get caught up in a superficial world.

You have spent your days trying something new
You have looked at magazine girls wishing they were you
Do you see in photographs an angel that once was you?
Does she tell you stories that are true?'

The song has a definite Far Eastern influence, and it's no wonder why it went down so well in Japan. After the quiet mid-section where the vocoder comes in once again, the song starts to build to something mysterious and intense, thanks to Palmer ratcheting up the tension ever so slowly with steadily increasing military snare drum that gets louder and louder. Then suddenly, the song cascades into a visceral explosion, with Wetton repeating the song title as Palmer gets fast and furious with lots of cymbals (including ride cymbal for dramatic accent), toms and bass drum. Howe unleashes his most furious soloing on the album, and Downes accompanies him with trade-off licks. But sadly, we have yet another fade that occurs at an inappropriate time.

Nonetheless, the band has concocted a masterpiece: a song that has lived in the setlist ever since, sometimes as the final encore. Lake commended himself quite well on the *Asia in Asia* concert, and John Payne did himself well on the song too. But it's Wetton that owns the song, and there are many great versions from the reunion era available. Also, no guitarist has played this song with that signature sound, but Howe and many have done a nice job trying.

Many fans complained that if *Alpha* could contain such a progressive gem, why not have more of this style? Well, because Geffen wanted hits and that's what the team of Downes and Wetton were going for. And remember that Asia wasn't created to be playing progressive rock epics, so it's nice that they decided to do a song like this. *Alpha* may not have been the album that *Asia* was, but it has aged fairly well, despite the mix issues, and by no means was it a flop musically or commercially.

As for the messy situation with Wetton leaving the band during the *Asian Invasion* tour, Howe told me this in our interview from 2001:

To be precise, there was a lot of unrest on the *Alpha* tour, and John sensed it, and then he actually left after he sensed that he was becoming the victim, if you like, in the band. There's very often the victim of the band, a victim of other people's disappointment or reliability and trust. You know, there was a lot of that being flaunted as opposed to being tightened up. We did get a bit gappy on that tour, so yes, we started to say to John, 'Oh, this is getting to be a problem'. He sensed a victimising, but he also felt he was the odd man out, and as far as I know, he officially left during that tour. And it seemed like that the only conclusion we could draw after that tour was, well, this isn't working as this four-piece lineup, and we have to get somebody else. So, it was really a – what do they call it – a run around the gooseberry bush? Whatever we did, didn't seem to be right. We had Greg Lake for a while and that didn't settle into a long term thing.

I then asked whether Lake was a good musical fit since the songs had to be readjusted with key changes and such, and Steve said;

Due to his vocal range and due to the fact that John found it hard to sing a lot of those songs on stage due to the key, Greg insisted we change the key on a lot of songs. So, you know, we didn't have too many choices of where to go. We were locked into Greg and we went with Greg for that period in late '83, but when that failed, John came back. John wanted to come back to Asia, and this is just before the 'Rock and Roll Dream' album (*Astra*).

And we all know that it would be a long, long time before the original lineup made amends and reunited.

Alpha Rarities
'Daylight' (Downes/Wetton)

'Daylight' is one of the best songs Asia ever recorded and has a very strange history. Initially, it was the B-side to the 'Don't Cry' single in the summer of 1983. Back in the good old days of radio, a lead single would usually be issued about a month in advance of the forthcoming album. Usually, the B-side was a non-album track, and sometimes FM radio stations would also play it since it was also a new song. That was the case with 'Daylight', and because it received so much airplay, it hit number 24 at Album Rock.

A perfect summer song, 'Daylight' encapsulates everything that was great about Asia: the melody, the arrangement, the production and the feel – all of which added up to a radio-ready hit. The song begins with church-like organ, and when Wetton's voice enters, it becomes even more spiritual. Once the drums and guitars kick in, it is pure exuberance. Palmer keeps his kick drum going as Wetton proclaims:

Daylight, I want to see daylight
Want to see daylight that shines all around
Daylight, I want to see clear blue light
Want to see daylight that shines all around

It is in-between these lines where Howe and Downes interlock in a gorgeous keyboard/guitar combination that sounds like vintage Yes. It even sounds like Howe is playing his guitars through a Leslie speaker, but that could just be the keyboards intertwining, giving it that watery sound. Either way, it's fantastic.

Each member shines on this song, and wisely, it was performed on the 1983 tour, both with Wetton and then Lake. Lake struggled with it, but let's face it, this is a tough one to sing and he did a decent job. But the song would not see 'daylight' again until the *Phoenix* tour in 2008 when it was used as the opener, and the audience loved it.

'Daylight' was initially included only on the cassette version of *Alpha,* and Wetton explained why: 'We were one of the biggest-bootlegged bands of all time. Estimates are two million bootlegs of home-taping or people selling it (*Asia*) on the street. We tried to do something to entice people to buy the cassette rather than to make their own cassette, so we put an extra track on the cassette that wasn't on the album'. The song would not be on the vinyl nor most of the CD copies, but it finally surfaced on the *Heat of the Moment* compilation in 2000.

'Lying To Yourself' (Howe/Wetton)

The only track from the *Alpha* sessions that Steve Howe received a co-writing credit for was this gem, which was used as a B-side for the 'The Smile Has Left Your Eyes' single. This is another song that would've made the *Alpha* album much better as a whole had it been included. 'Lying to Yourself' is well-crafted pop/rock, with some subtle yet sophisticated touches. Palmer's drum mix sounds leagues better than it did on the album, and the song sounds like it could've deserved a place on the debut. Perhaps that's why it was nixed from *Alpha*. But really, it's a mystery why this song didn't make the cut. Was it because Steve wrote most of it? There is a demo from around 1981 that has Steve working on the track by himself, and you can hear the genesis of the song.

This mid-tempo number has some great hooks and arrangements and it's superior to, say, 'True Colours' or 'Never in a Million Years'. The guitar solo soars, as do the rhythm guitar and drumming behind it. It certainly stands out as a viable track, but record label and band politics probably doomed it to B-side status. Thankfully, this track would also appear on the *Heat of the Moment* compilation.

'Jodie' (Downes/Wetton)

This remains an unreleased track from the album sessions. Downes was quoted as saying, 'That song was written by myself and John Wetton. It was never totally finished. It was vocalised but didn't get the same injection that the other tracks got. Steve did a basic rhythm track, but I don't think he ever really got into it'. When the *Alpha* demos leaked online, this track wasn't included. However, 25 years later, it would be reworked as 'Alibis' on the 2008 reunion album *Phoenix*, where it turned out to be a very nice song after all.

Astra (1985)

Personnel:
John Wetton: bass, vocals
Mandy Meyer: guitars
Geoff Downes: keyboards
Carl Palmer: drums
Additional musicians: The Royal Philharmonic Orchestra on 'Rock and Roll Dream', conducted and arranged by Louis Clark.
Released: 15 November 1985
Recorded: Westside Studios (London, UK), Townhouse (London, UK), Sarm West Studios (London, UK) September 1984-July 1985
Producers: Mike Stone and Geoff Downes
Engineers: Mike Stone, Alan Douglas
Cover Illustration: Roger Dean
Highest Chart Position: UK: 67, US: 68, Canada: 66, Japan: 15, Germany: 48, Switzerland: 10

At the summer 1983 release of Asia's previous studio album, the musical climate was very different from the one they returned to in late 1985. The band had been through several personnel changes and had taken an inordinate amount of time working on their next album. By the time that album – *Astra* – arrived in November 1985, many fans had moved on.

This was a sad thing because, in many ways, *Astra* is one of the best albums Asia ever made. John Wetton himself said so, and this author agrees. Quite a few fans do indeed love this album, but also there are those who felt it did not deliver. Critics, for the most part, remained pretty savage, although, in some corners, there were positive reviews. Speaking of Wetton, he returned to the band in early 1984 after Lake departed, and though some bitter feelings had to be smoothed over, Wetton brought with him some new songs that he was preparing for a possible solo album.

Work began around February/March 1984, with Mike Stone producing. In interviews at the time, it seemed clear that Wetton belonged back in the band but that there was still confusion over who forced him out in the first place (most theories lead to a combination of management and record label executives). In an interview at the time with *Request* magazine, Wetton said, 'I was quite happy with the way things were going in a kind of pop/rock direction, and when I got kicked out, I couldn't understand why. Nobody told me what happened or what I'd done wrong. But no one ever said that to me, and I still don't know to this day why everything went the way that it did'.

Downes and Palmer were happy to have John back, as Palmer told *Hit Parader*: 'A lot of decisions were made by the record company. We had a very interesting contract. The reason John was brought back into the band was they – and thank God they did – owned up that they had made a drastic mistake. This was the singer and that was it, and to try and bring in somebody who sounded like him was silly'.

As for Downes, his writing partner was now back, and he wanted it that way and told *Hit Parader*: 'I wanted to carry on working with John. I wrote some stuff and got John to sing on it, and we took songs to Brian Lane. We played them to him. I think 'Rock and Roll Dream' was one of them. I think that convinced him that if we were to carry on as Asia, John had to come back in. This is approximately February/March 1984. We had a meeting with Steve, Carl and Brian Lane and decided to go in and do some more substantial demos'.

Alas, things would not work out as hoped. Howe and Wetton could not get along, and really, that was no shock. I asked Howe about this time period in our interview from 2001, and he told me:

We were working on *Astra* for about two weeks together, all of us, and I thought that we found that germ again, you know, that the germ of Asia was happening. We started to have a good time with the *Astra* material, but then suddenly, John really upped himself. He said 'No, no, this isn't working'. I was aghast because I thought it was. So, that's how the confrontation came where John said, 'Well, I can't work with Steve'. I said, 'I really don't understand why not. We were having a great time in the studio. What's going on?' I guess the band backed John at that point. So I left with a smile on my face and wished them luck. What we learned was that you really can't change the singer in a band very easily, and mostly you can't change anybody in a band if it's reliant on such stylistic potential.

I asked Howe if he ever heard *Astra*, and he told me:

Yeah, well you know, there are things they might not want me to tell you, but basically, I heard it in a big way because I heard the initial two weeks of recording it. Then I guess you could say I got fired! I was then off doing GTR, and Asia actually invited me back to play guitar on the record and I agreed. Then they sent me some material and I said, 'No, I can't do this!'. I liked the idea, but I couldn't bring myself to commit to work through all of the material they had. So, unwisely, they didn't just play me the skeleton of the album; they played me a huge wad of material at the time that, to me, was flat and dull and unexciting. I think *Astra* ended up better than what I had heard.

So, in September 1984, Howe was gone, and the band began a seemingly endless search for a new guitarist. At one point, they discussed using an all-star cast of different players, such as David Gilmour of Pink Floyd, Jeff Beck, and Brian May of Queen. But wisely, they ended up acquiring a permanent member instead in Mandy Meyer: a Swiss guitarist who had played with hard rock outfits Cobra and Krokus. Meyer was an odd choice considering his background, but he fit in fantastically.

In an MTV interview with Meyer and Wetton from around December 1985, Meyer was asked how he got into the band: 'It was John Kalodner of Geffen Records who recommended me to the band and set up an audition, and that's how we met'. Wetton then chimed in, saying, 'It wasn't really an audition. Actually, he just came with us and played for a couple of days and we were convinced. We were prepared to go into the studio as a three-piece and just make the record the way we wanted to with guest guitar players, but then Mandy came along and he seemed to fit in so well, he was invited to become a full member'.

MTV VJ Mark Goodman, then asked Wetton what happened with Steve Howe, and Wetton tackled the thorny subject as such: 'Well, it was almost a prerequisite of my rejoining the band that Steve left. We were always at opposite ends of the scale musically. He was pulling in a totally different direction from me, and basically, if you listen to this album, this is exactly what I wanted to do, and it wouldn't have been what Steve Howe wanted to do'.

Then asked what had kept Asia together through all of the recent changes, Wetton answered, 'Basically, underneath it all, we like each other. We may not show it most of the time, but we do like each other, and there's something important about this band. When we started out in 1981, we had a lot to prove, like we weren't over the hill and we could still write good songs and be a recording entity, and throughout all the problems that we've had, we still want to play together'.

As for the impressive album cover design, Wetton said, 'Roger Dean would be better qualified to tell you, but basically it's an equivalent story to Adam and Eve, and Aza (the female robot on the cover) is a fallen angel who fell to Earth and was the equivalent of Eve eating the apple. It all takes place in a place called Arcadia, which is a Greek mythological place, and the fallen angel is in fact, this female robot from the 21st century'.

When asked about the proposed tour for 1986, Meyer said, 'We are looking at next spring, maybe March. I really feel comfortable actually and it's nice. It took a few months for us to get used to each other musically, but after that, it was all good'. Wetton added, 'We're still talking to a lot of different people about what you will see on this tour. It's going to be so different from the last time we went out... or 'they' went out (laughs). It's going to have to be phenomenal, I think'.

Sadly, none of this would come to be, as Geffen bailed on the band in 1986 and Asia quietly disbanded. I think a tour for *Astra* would've been something special, and it's rather shocking how Geffen pulled the plug after Asia had been such a huge success for them.

The album took an eternity to make, however. Mike Stone was back as producer (although the band did meet with Martin Rushent of Human League/ XTC/Joy Division fame), but that didn't pan out. Stone commented on why he returned: 'They asked! Mandy came in and the whole band quieted down a bit. At the end, it became like, "Let's get this done".

The band had 20-25 songs: an insane amount and enough for a double album. But it took far too long to decide the direction, what songs should stay or go, and how the mixing process should be. Stone had to leave after about six months, so Downes took over for the last four months. Not only that, they had to change the album title from *Arcadia* to *Astra*, because a Duran Duran offshoot project called Arcadia was due to release their album at the exact same time.

So much time had been wasted, and by late 1985, the music scene had changed drastically, bringing huge acts including Tears For Fears, U2, Madonna, Prince, Howard Jones, Simple Minds and INXS. Also, Marillion had now become the most popular progressive band of the 1980s. Asia had a huge mountain to climb, and quite simply, a large portion of the population had forgotten about them, which was a real shame.

'Go' (Downes/Wetton)

Once again, like the first two albums, Asia chose the opening track as the first single. As with those albums, it was also the last song written for the album. 'Go' reintroduced Asia to the marketplace in a bold way.

The track begins with a combination of organ and icy synths from Downes. Palmer bashes in with programmed-sounding single snare drum hits that were in fact, the clatter of his new Yamaha kit. Meyer's guitars enter with harmonies, the first verse then chugging along staccato-style with a hard rock edge. The choruses are explosive, with Wetton's shouting of 'Get up and go!' echoing as the guitars, keyboards and drums kick it up a notch. Simply put, this is a rocker built for arenas, and it has a futuristic feel, much like Roger Dean's album cover illustration.

After a screeching note high up the guitar neck, Meyer's mid-section solo gives way to Downes' crystalline synth breaks. Behind all this, Palmer pummels his snare before switching over to tom patterns as Meyer takes over for a second solo, involving some clever double-tracking and harmonies. Eventually, Palmer rips off a snare roll that segues into meaty power chords showing Meyer's hard rock/metal chops. The final verse follows. The song's ending has stinging leads throughout, and just before the last part of the fade, Palmer gives a double-kick exhibition.

US radio responded, sending 'Go' to number 7 at Album Rock, charting for thirteen weeks. Despite heavy MTV rotation and being an MTV exclusive in November and December, the single would fall just shy of the Top 40, peaking at 46.

The music video looked nothing short of spectacular, as Roger Dean's fantastical, futuristic album cover came to life, as did the female on the cover, Aza, who even took a shower in the video. Directed by Peter Christopherson, the band looked great in the video, although Wetton's hair was a mess, making it look like he just woke up. Palmer's new Yamaha kit was cool indeed, having a bizarre set of toms with what looked like jungle tribesman's heads. Most of the guys looked snazzy in casual suit jackets, and the awesome lighting and design were much updated from the last time the band toured. This was supposed to give fans an idea of what was to come for the 1986 tour, which was sadly scrapped, as mentioned earlier.

Asked what the song was about, Wetton didn't seem to know and was quoted in an interview on his website: 'That is the only song that I can't explain what it's about. 'Go' was just an elite experiment. It just so happened that the record company chose it to be the single. I can give you a million reasons why we wrote 'Voice of America' and 'Rock and Roll Dream', but I have absolutely nothing to say about 'Go''.

'Go' has been a big live number over the years. The track was first played live on the *Then and Now* tour and was a great vehicle for Pat Thrall's guitar chops in 1990. In the Howe era, the song started being performed on the *Omega* tour in 2010, and though Steve's sound is ill-suited to a song like this, at least he was game to play it. This popular song has been on virtually every Asia compilation, but bizarrely, was left off of *Then and Now*.

'Voice Of America' (Downes/Wetton)

This song meant quite a lot to John Wetton and was one of the tracks he wrote when pondering a possible solo album before returning to the band. 'Voice of America' was his salute to the music that enraptured him as a youngster growing up and hearing what American radio he could. Wetton was a big fan of the Beach Boys, and we can hear that acknowledgement with this song.

'Voice of America' has some pretty melodies and arrangements and would not have been out of place on *Alpha*. The opening minute is simply Downes on piano and keyboards, accompanied by Wetton singing his story line. Meyer and Palmer join in for the first chorus, and the song soars from there. Both Meyer and Palmer's playing was so sympathetic to the song, never outreaching it, that it was a credit to the writing.

Before the guitar solo, lovely vocal harmonies right out of the Beach Boys songbook accompany Downes' harpsichord-playing. After another chorus, Meyer lays down a perfectly-executed solo, concluding with a final held note, as Palmer does a brief drum fill, the chorus then taking us out.

An outstanding track, it is mind-boggling that Geffen wouldn't have sent this to radio or issued it as a single. Wetton felt so strongly about the track that it was included in preference to 'Go' on *Then and Now*, and was performed on that tour. John Payne paid respect to the song on the *Aqua* tour, but it didn't last the whole set of shows. But it did return as an acoustic number on the *Phoenix* tour. This is an extremely important song in the Asia canon.

'Hard On Me' (Downes/Palmer/Wetton)

No question about it, 'Hard On Me' is a straightforward pop song that gets right in the listener's head and stays there. In the writing phase, it was a late addition. A warm, infectious tune, it's perhaps a little too lightweight for most Asia fans and certainly for progressive rock fans, but it is insistent and as catchy as can be.

All the instruments have nice separation and Wetton's bass is prominent in the mix. John sings with verve, and Downes has some playful keyboard parts, including the intro. Meyer's lead guitar in the middle acts as more of a fill than a solo. The muted, driving guitar parts on the verses are effective, as are the guitar fills during the breaks.

A cheesy hand-clap effect and some dated mid-1980s drum treatments aside, this is an enjoyable listen. Is it an essential track? No, but it's a pleasant one. The song came into being late in the sessions as Geffen demanded a single, and yet it wasn't chosen as a single. More record company genius in action! This track was never played live.

'Wishing' (Downes/Wetton)

Now here's a song that easily could've been a smash. 'Wishing' has some of the best melodies that the pair of Downes and Wetton ever came up with. This was one of the songs that Wetton composed before rejoining the band when he was thinking of doing a solo album.

The song has a different structure in that it basically starts with the chorus (after a lovely keyboard introduction which pans the sound speaker-to-speaker). Where the chorus would normally go, we basically get a pre-chorus, or in this case, a second chorus. The song hooks the listener in immediately, and the balance of keyboards, a steady drum rhythm, and a thematic guitar solo emulating some of the vocal lines add up to a great listen.

Wetton's vocals are top-notch, and it's hard to understand how Geffen wouldn't see a hit here, especially after all the time and money spent on crafting the album. A promo single was pressed in 1986, but the single itself never materialised, as Geffen pulled all promotion after the album got off to a slow start. But many fans are fond of this track, and it has appeared on compilations with good reason. 'Wishing' was never performed live, which is a real shame. Somebody with talent and taste needs to cover this someday and give it the audience it deserves.

'Rock And Roll Dream' (Downes/Wetton)

And here we have the longest song in Asia's career up to this point. Clocking in at just under seven minutes, 'Rock And Roll Dream' – accompanied by the Royal Philharmonic Orchestra conducted by Louis Clark – is an epic that has a full, rich sound and arrangement. Clark was a familiar name to rock fans through his orchestral work with acts such as Ozzy Osbourne and the Electric Light Orchestra.

Although no fan wants to hear a rich rock star moan about how life can be a struggle, the truth is, the rock lifestyle is not all it's cracked up to be. The lyrics detail this in a relatable way, especially with the chorus where it states, 'Rock and roll dream, Not what it seems, Who is the dreamer now?'. This interesting line seems to be saying that although many fans dream of the limos, private jets, screaming fans and parties, the rock stars may be dreaming of a nine-to-five job, watching sports on TV, taking the dog for a walk or the kids to a movie – in other words, normalcy.

41

As for the music, the song has loads of voices on the chorus (all Wetton) and several different parts. One of the key things about this song is that it never feels long or overstays its welcome. After an a capella chorus opens the song, the moody verses begin with subtle keyboards, programmed handclaps and occasional guitar licks from Meyer. Once the guitars and drums come in, the song takes a heavier, more ominous tone, and Palmer switches to a steady beat before the bouncy piano lines enter, summoning up the glorious full chorus for the first time.

Meyer then rips off a thematic solo adorned with crowd noise for effect. Another set of verses follow and then it's off to the chorus again with that amazing piano line, but this time, the orchestra joins in. A set of choruses with just drums and vocals follows (you can just tell this was built for the stage), and then Meyer gives forth a series of infectious riffs followed by another brilliant solo as the orchestra swirls all around. More choruses come with the orchestra now in full swing. The last two minutes or so go this way, with strings eventually playing the melody as Wetton's voice begins to fade.

This breathtaking song ranks highly in the Asia repertoire. It would get played live for the first time on the 1990-1991 tour and sounded pretty damn good with Pat Thrall on guitar on *Live in Moscow*. The band also played a fantastic version on the *Aqua* tour, where US audiences got to hear it live for the first time. It hasn't been played on tour since. 'Rock And Roll Dream' is a special piece of music.

'Countdown To Zero' (Downes/Wetton)

The Cold War and threat of nuclear war were topical in the mid-1980s, and many bands wrote about them. Sometimes this could yield interesting results, and sometimes not. With 'Countdown To Zero', the band took an awkward step. It's not that the song lacked good ideas, but there were some ill-advised and heavy-handed moments that just didn't work.

The song opens side two of the original vinyl with a famous sound sample called 'Deep Note', that was created by a man named Andy Moorer. You've heard this sound at every movie theatre that is THX-enabled, as well as on any home system. It's the same exact thing on the Asia song. Without knowing about 'Deep Note', I asked Geoff back in 2003 if the sound was Asia's and if they got any royalties. He told me it was from a found sample and it wasn't theirs, but that he couldn't remember the guy's name. Now we know!

As for the song itself, it relies on a lot of techno-clatter, with layers of keyboards, punchy bass notes, and odd-sounding guitars that are very clean with little-to-no distortion. A fairly preposterous spoken-word part has Wetton pleading:

Don't do it, don't do it
Don't start the countdown to zero
We want to live, We want to live

We will live
You've got your finger on the trigger
Take it off, let it go
Let it pass, let it go

Nonetheless, it does create an ominous mood, and on early CD pressings, the digital track time readout would hit fifteen seconds and would then do a countdown to zero. Although this was never played live by Asia, Wetton and Downes did play it at some iCon shows. Though it didn't sound quite right without the technology, it was still neat to hear it in a concert setting.

'Love Now Till Eternity' (Downes/Wetton)
This is a very pretty song and one that sounds as though it could've been on a movie soundtrack. Downes' orchestral keyboard sounds employed in the opening offer a regal feel, and Wetton sings with the utmost class.

Geoff gets some of his very best piano sounds on this album, and that is evident on this song. John's vocals – harmonising with himself – are also quite exquisite. Palmer drums with total class and restraint, although there's too much reverb utilized. After the second set of choruses, the instrumental break with the orchestral keyboards comes in, this time accompanied by excellent guitar harmonies from Meyer. The rest of the track develops into one long repetition of choruses, but not before Meyer strums delicately, almost sounding like a mandolin or mandola, as Wetton sings the pretty 'Love now' refrain.

Palmer brings it back up with a drum fill, and the song plays out from there. While this is a beautiful song, it may have worked better on a Wetton solo album. One can't help but think of *Alpha* when hearing this song which is on the softer side of things.

'Too Late' (Downes/Palmer/Wetton)
This icy rocker cranks up the volume on *Astra* for sure. The verses are dark and heavy, with beefy power chords from Meyer, while Downes' keyboard textures float amongst the stop/start rhythms. Palmer throws in thrusting double-kick pedal action, and that is probably why he got a co-writing credit, though I'm just guessing.

This song shares many similarities with Bon Jovi's 'Runaway' from 1984, Michael Bolton's'Fool's Game' from 1983, and 1982's 'Fantasy', a classic by Aldo Nova. See what I'm getting at here? Those percolating keyboard breaks have been a staple of AOR hard rock songs, especially in the 1980s. But it works just fine here, and the song adds some balls to the album.

Meyer not only has a ripping solo, but he also tosses in a seriously funky breakdown at the 1:10 mark. It's brief but really stands out and is quite different for the band. The choruses are strong, and the gothic opening vocals are Wetton magic.

43

'Too Late' was aptly titled, as it was issued as a promo single to rock radio in January 1986, making it to number 30 on the Album Rock charts in the US. It was indeed too late, as Asia had more or less disbanded at that point, though that wasn't official just yet. But with no tour and no more MTV videos, it was obvious Geffen had stopped promoting the album. The song was played live only on the 1989 European dates by Wetton and Palmer with session men.

'Suspicion' (Downes/Wetton)

Here's an odd one. 'Suspicion' is one of the more obscure tracks from the classic Asia years. There is a mysterious mood hanging over this song and it is also a touch macabre. Downes creates the unsettling atmosphere with his exotic mixture of keyboard sounds. The lyrics deal with mistrust, perhaps even jealousy, and something darker.

What exactly is going on is unclear, but it is eerie. The song is largely downbeat until a snaky synthesizer solo from Downes, which is really his only synth solo on the album. The bridge follows and is fairly powerful, being the only time the track gets lively with some guitars and drums. The track then drops back down into the dark mood, concluding with the lyrics, 'Where were you yesterday? Where will you be tomorrow?'.

After that last line of lyrics, only Palmer's drums are heard, with subtle rimshots that just fade out. It's effective, but the song feels like more could've been fleshed out of it. It's certainly different and not without appeal. 'Suspicion' was never played live.

'After The War' (Downes/Wetton)

Astra concludes with the mini-epic, 'After the War', which is a dynamic number rivaling anything from the debut album. After a quiet piano introduction, Palmer assaults his drums in that familiar military style, while Downes supplies an arsenal of cinematic, symphonic keyboard sounds.

The verses continue to thrust with attack, and the pre-chorus is quite elegant-sounding until the crashing power chords of the chorus. Palmer's best drumming on the album is right here, and Wetton offers his best bass-playing as well: something that really took a back seat on the album as a whole.

Around the 3:40 mark – after a thudding Palmer fill – Meyer crafts a splendid guitar solo with skill, precision and taste, and also adds more eloquent double-tracked guitar harmonies. It's stunning work. Then Meyer plays some beautiful classical guitar as Wetton sings the final lyrics, which end with a crashing chord.

Fans of the progressive rock that Asia came from were probably pleased with this number and 'Rock And Roll Dream', but little else. The album was worked-on entirely too long, but it really was a work of art. When it didn't break out right away, Geffen panicked and abandoned the band. It's truly a shame because *Astra* was an excellent piece of work that deserved a far better fate. Asia quietly disbanded in early 1986. The tour – which was to have kicked off in Europe in the spring, following through North America in the summer – was scrapped due to lack of label support.

Mandy Meyer was outstanding on this record, and his playing sounds fresh to this day. He's never done better work, and he's had a pretty nice career, having gone on to play with country-rockers Stealin' Horses as well as House of Lords, unsuccessful short-lived supergroup (and John Kalodner creation) Katmandu, Swiss hard rockers, Gotthard, and now once again, Krokus.

Astra Rarities
'Go' (remix) (Downes/Wetton)
Geffen suggested that Asia join the many artists who were now releasing extended remixes. 'Go', as the lead single, was the obvious choice. It was decided to leave the remix in the hands of Geoff Downes, and it was made available only on the UK 12" release. The results are mixed – pun intended. Actually, it's pretty cool in some spots, and since it was made for the clubs and the DJs, it was well over seven minutes in length.

Some new parts were added in, including percussion by Luis Jardim, who would also appear on the *Arena* and *Aura* albums. Jardim is a famed percussionist from his work with ABC, Grace Jones, Seal, Duran Duran, Coldplay and more. His first wife was the female singer on The Buggles' classic 'Video Killed the Radio Star?', and that's how Downes met Jardim.

Downes throws in a cool organ solo on the remix as well. Long sought-after, this version was included on *The Definitive Collection* in 2006 – the only place it appears on CD to this day.

'Am I In Love?' (Downes/Wetton)
This song ended up appearing on *Then and Now* and is covered on that album in the compilation section.

Aurora EP (1986)
Highest Chart Position: Japan: 66

At one time, this was the rarest of all Asia releases. A Japan-only EP, *Aurora* featured four tracks, with 'Too Late' – the second single from the then-current *Astra* LP – as the lead cut. The other tracks were the rare B-sides, 'Ride Easy', 'Daylight' and 'Lying To Yourself'. If you didn't have the vinyl 45 single releases, then you could only find the B-sides on this release. This used to go for a pretty good amount of money back in the day, and it is still a quite rare vinyl collector's item.

The three B-sides finally made their CD debut on the 2000 compilation album, *The Very Best of Asia: Heat of the Moment (1982-1990)*. The cover featured Roger Dean's logo, with a design by Yasutaka Kato.

Aqua (1992)

Personnel:
John Payne: bass, vocals, guitars
Al Pitrelli: guitars
Steve Howe: acoustic guitars, pedal steel guitars, dobro, mandolin
Geoff Downes: keyboards, backing vocals
Carl Palmer: drums. percussion
Additional musicians: Anthony Glynne (guitars), Simon Phillips (drums), Nigel Glockler (drums), Michael Sturgis (drums)
Released: 8 June 1992 (Europe and Japan), 15 September 1992 (US)
Recorded: Advision Studios (Brighton, UK) July 1991-April 1992
Producer: Geoff Downes
Engineer: Pete Craigie
Cover Illustration: Rodney Matthews
Highest Chart Position: Japan: 21, Germany: 51, Switzerland: 20

We now enter the beginning of a new era for Asia. The band reformed officially in 1990, with Wetton, Downes and Palmer that summer issuing *Then and Now*: a 'comeback' and greatest hits album including four alleged new songs. Prior to the 1990-1991 world, the band added ex-Automatic Man, Pat Travers Band and Hughes/Thrall guitarist Pat Thrall – the first American to join Asia.

The tour produced the concert album, *Live In Moscow*. But by the time of its 1991 issue, Wetton had already left for a solo career. Thrall would also soon depart (to join Meat Loaf's band), and Palmer agreed to an ELP reunion, leaving Downes as the lone Asia member.

Geoff decided to go forward, bringing in bassist/vocalist/guitarist John Payne, who had done demos with Downes in the past and had briefly been with Electric Light Orchestra Part II. Payne was an obscure choice but a talented guy who was up for the challenge of being the new Asia frontman. He relayed his story as to how it all happened in David Gallant's book on Asia:

I got a call from one of Geoff's managing partners, Harry Cowell, to come down to Nomis Studios, where Geoff had been doing some of his work – I think with Glenn Hughes at the time. I sat down with him and his manager and said, 'What's going on?'. I remember I even took my cat to the meeting. I had this Siamese cat named Eric. He used to come with me everywhere. So I went to Nomis with all these bands rehearsing there, and here I have this cat.

So Geoff said to me, 'How do you fancy joining Asia?', and I said, "Well, that's a bit of a heavy one to throw at somebody!". Of course, I said, "Yeah, but who's going to play bass?". He said, 'Well, you are!'. I said, "I've only played bass on demos; I've never played bass and sung at the same time".

I've played guitar for years and sung. I've played bass loads of times and sung loads of times, but never the two together. I then embarked on months of singing and playing together, which was a nightmare because it was quite a hard thing to do. Especially if you've got the two things in different time registers. But eventually, after about three or four months, it clicked.

The new guitarist was axe-shredder Al Pitrelli, formerly with Alice Cooper (he was Alice's musical director from 1989-1991) and Widowmaker. Palmer was onboard to start the album, but could not finish the project and appeared on only three songs. Other drummers used to complete the sessions were ex-Saxon and GTR drummer Nigel Glockler, Michael Sturgis who had played with Phenomena and A-ha (and almost with Asia in 1987) and the legendary Simon Phillips (of Toto, Pete Townshend and Jeff Beck fame). During the sessions, Steve Howe, surprisingly, returned. So, in the end, it was marketed as being a five-man lineup, with three-quarters of the original band in Downes, Howe and Palmer, although that was not quite accurate.

The end result was *Aqua*: the first studio album from the band in seven long years. Downes produced the album, and the cover illustration was a brilliant design by Rodney Matthews. *Aqua* was a slick, very commercial, harder-rocking version of the band that bore little resemblance to the normal sound, look and feel of Asia. Many fans refused to support the new lineup without Wetton, and others gave it a shot but did not care for the slicker hard rock. Other fans found the album to be quite likeable and a nice change. There wasn't much in the way of middle ground.

The band was now on independent labels (Great Pyramid in the US and Musidisc in the UK and Europe) and could not be guaranteed any airplay or decent promotional push. On top of that, many casual music fans considered Asia to be a dated 1980s relic, and there was little chance critics would suddenly be on the band's side. Considering all that was against it, *Aqua* did reasonably well – not well enough to reach either the US or UK charts, but sales were around 250,000 copies. The record did decently in Japan, nearly reaching the Top 20, and charted in Germany and Switzerland.

As for the lengthy 1992-1993 tour, Asia would now play venues that were in the 1,000-3,000 capacity range, but usually closer to 1,000. The touring lineup was Downes, Payne, Howe, former Dare guitarist Vinny Burns, and drummer Trevor Thornton. The shows were very strong, mixing new and old material quite well, although Howe wouldn't come onstage until after five or six songs from both *Astra* and *Aqua* that he had nothing to do with.

The final leg of the tour took place in Eastern Europe in the fall of 1993, by which point Howe (later to return to Yes) and Burns had left, with Keith More of Arena filling in on guitar. Payne acquitted himself quite well on the tour, despite that awful top hat. However you look at it, it was a new era for Asia, and not without its rewards.

'Aqua Part 1' (Downes/Howe/Payne)
Aqua opens in excellent fashion with, of all things, the first piece of instrumental music in Asia's history. 'Aqua Part 1' is a beautiful classical guitar

piece from Howe, played elegantly over new age keyboard chords supplied by Downes, accompanied by crashing ocean waves.

Howe has composed tons of instrumental acoustic and classical pieces in his career, but this stands the test of time as one of his very best. It was also the song that Howe would play each night on the *Aqua* tour, as he took to the stage to rapturous applause. This is one of the few progressive rock moments on the album, and it was a quality beginning to the Payne era.

'Who Will Stop The Rain?' (Downes/Warman/Woolfenden)

The first song that fans got to hear John Payne sing for Asia was absolutely amazing. If only the majority of *Aqua* could've reached this level. 'Who Will Stop The Rain?' has all the Asia hallmarks: impressive musicianship, stellar production, fantastic melodies and impressive arrangements. The song originated in the late 1980s during the Rain demos with Max Bacon, and was radically reworked here.

The opening keyboard sequence sets things up perfectly, the insistent keyboard riff with hard-edged guitars then coming in followed by the chorus. Once the verses kick in, Payne's talent is obvious from his impassioned singing. The vocal layers in the choruses are fantastic, and the environmentally-conscious lyrics are, for the most part, really well done and easily the best on the album. The ending verse is excellent and seems to be a tribute to environmental protectors such as Greenpeace: 'There is no sense in turning back, To wash the debris from the track, World without fears without rhyme, We fought for peace within our time'.

This song is very well-constructed and is a perfect mix of progressive rock and commercially accessible pop/rock. There are two guitar solos. The first is Howe playing an expertly picked acoustic solo, perhaps on a twelve-string. This gives the song some Yes qualities leading to the bridge, which is really a reprisal of the opening. The second solo, towards the end of the song, is quite a ripping one from Pitrelli that involves typical hard rock moves and a bit of shredding. But it is tastefully done and adds some modern bite to the song.

It's a mystery who plays drums on what tracks on some of *Aqua*, but this is Michael Sturgis on drums as this song originated on the Rain demos, and he played on those pieces.

'Who Will Stop The Rain?' could've been the comeback hit they needed, but in typical Asia fashion, it got botched. There were plans for a video, but the label couldn't fund it in the end. The song did get some radio play in the US for a few weeks (I personally heard it at least three times here in the Philadelphia area), but Pyramid Records just didn't put enough of a promotional push behind it financially.

The label did take out a full-page ad in *Billboard* when *Aqua* came out in the US in the fall of '92, but it was such a tough time for a band like Asia to compete with Nirvana, Alice in Chains, Smashing Pumpkins and the Red Hot Chili Peppers ruling the airwaves. Regardless, this song remains one of the best any lineup of Asia ever recorded, and it was in every set list in the Payne era.

'Back In Town' (Downes, Payne)

Quite a few tracks on *Aqua* were chasing an already dated sound, and 'Back In Town' is a blatant example. This song features such lyrics as, 'The bad boy's back, The bad boy's back, The bad boy's back in town, Don't you shoot him down'. Not every song has to be Bob Dylan lyrically, but this is quite sophomoric.

Howe opens the track with an acoustic slide solo for about ten seconds, and that's where his contribution ends. Pitrelli lays down a wah-wah guitar solo that is a bit of fun, Simon Phillips pounds in some of his classic double-kick pedal fills, and Downes uses an organ sound that gives a smidgen of a Deep Purple sound. So not all of it is a waste, but these are minute highlights at best.

The band did play this live each night, and it rocked enough, but the songwriting was too weak to take seriously. That being said, the song does rock and that seemed to be the point.

'Love Under Fire' (Downes/Lake)

Here is an absolutely lovely song that came from the Ride The Tiger demos between Downes and Greg Lake around 1989. No record deal came of it, but some of the songs surfaced, such as this one on *Aqua,* and another pretty song: 'Affairs of the Heart', which would appear on the Emerson, Lake & Palmer album, *Black Moon*, later that same year of 1992.

'Love Under Fire' has an attractive melody, and Downes shows first-class playing here, with perfectly-chosen keyboard chords and piano fills. Simon Phillips is as excellent as always on drums and Al Pitrelli delivers his best solo on the album, and it is very concise. There is an elegance about this song and it creates a great setting. It went down very well in concert and fitted in nicely with the classic Asia material: no surprise with a song co-written by Greg Lake.

John Payne avoids the vocal histrionics on this one, and that goes a long way to giving the song some extra class compared to a lot of the others. His vocals stay fairly close to the demo version from Ride the Tiger and really excel on this song, showing how good a choice he was for Asia.

One negative, though, is in the lyrics department. Lines such as 'You can hide in the jungle, You can climb up a tree, You can scan the horizon, Tell me, what do you see?' are so goofy that it almost harms the song. The music and melody save the day, however, and 'Love Under Fire' is indeed a winner.

'Someday' (Downes/Warman)

This one is really generic and is another of the kind of over-produced AOR/pop-metal that typifies Alias, Warrant, Slaughter and similar bands. Payne goes into overdrive with the vocals, especially on the sickly chorus. Downes tries to save the song with his classic synths in the bridge, but the sounds are too tender.

If you are a fan of this style of AOR, then it is well done for what it is, but this sound – hopelessly dated by 1992 – is just not Asia.

Once again, Steve Howe appears briefly, coming out of nowhere at the end to play a brief flamenco acoustic guitar part to the fade, which was clearly tacked on as if to say, 'Hey, Steve is on this one too!'. It's Michael Sturgis on drums on this track incidentally, as this was another song that originated from the Rain demos.

'Someday' was played live on every show of the tour, and the band were very pleased with this song. This is one of the slicker moments on the album that strays too far from the traditional sound and writing expected of Asia.

'Little Rich Boy' (Downes/Payne)
The song title alone should have any fan worry, and in fact, the US label Pyramid Records thought so too, deciding not to include it on the album. It was on the UK, Japanese and European release, however, and thus it will be reviewed here.

'Little Rich Boy' starts off with this lyrical gem: 'Don't read Marx, He's a clean-cut guy, Just the dream on a TV eye'. Marx? Are we talking about Groucho, Karl or even Richard Marx?

Simon Phillips does his best on drums, and the song certainly cranks the amps, but there's nothing much to recommend here. The band played it live and it came out fairly heavy, but it was still the same song and the same result.

At the end of the song in concert, Payne would trade-off solos on lead guitar (he played a double-neck with a bass and a guitar on this song) with Geoff on organ, at least offering some decency. Again, this wasn't remotely close to anything that would've been recorded under the Asia name before.

'The Voice Of Reason' (Downes/Payne)
Now this is more like it: Asia doing progressive rock in their own melodic style and doing it well. There are many reasons why this song is so good, and one of the most important factors is that Downes, Howe and Palmer are on it. Payne does a great job vocally, and the lyrics actually have a bit of depth, which is something you can't say about many of the songs on *Aqua*.

The first three minutes of 'The Voice Of Reason' are truly excellent. Howe plays an assortment of acoustic guitar, dobro, mandolin and pedal steel guitar in a haunting fashion. Payne joins in, very restrained vocally, but sings with conviction. When the drums and keyboards join in, the mood changes and the song gets more punch. Palmer's drumming is the same tight, no-nonsense approach that he used from the mid-1980s on, his drums very well-recorded and mixed.

The song's close sees Palmer switching up to the military snare style he does so well, as Downes adds layers of keyboard fills and the song marches to its grand conclusion at the 5:37 mark. This is one song you wish could've been even longer. It was performed on the *Aqua* tour but sadly was dropped early on in the North American leg, never to be played again. This is a highly recommended song and proof that the guys had the capability of writing classic-sounding Asia material.

'Lay Down Your Arms' (Downes/Payne/Hart)

Don't always believe filmmakers. Asia would painfully learn that lesson with 'Lay Down Your Arms'. One of the best songs on *Aqua*, it ended up in the abysmal animated debacle, *Freddie as F.R.O.7*, which earned the honour of lowest-grossing animated film of all-time!

Payne hilariously detailed this amphibian failure in David Gallant's book on Asia:

This was the biggest animation ever done in the UK. Unfortunately, it was crap. It was about a cartoon frog. It got to the stage where we mixed it in Dolby Surround Sound, and the film guy comes up to me and says, 'I like it when it gets to the chorus. Can you add a little bit to the chorus where you sing the phrase, 'And Freddie says lay down your arms'?'. They tried and tried to get me to do this, but I just refused. It was bad enough having music in a film about a little green frog!

The song itself goes along at a decent pace and picks up with a beautiful chorus, although the many layers of backing vocals become distracting. The Eddie Van Halen-styled guitar parts are acceptable and subtle during the verses, and the drumming is appropriate, and most likely Nigel Glockler. The bridge is vintage Asia, and Geoff Downes puts forth another keyboard solo with those bold, familiar synth sounds. He also throws in some piano licks here and there, including during the song's fade-out. 'Lay Down Your Arms' was a very good live number that slotted in well with the classic Asia material. Freddie the Frog would've been very hoppy.

'Crime Of The Heart' (Downes/Warman)

John Payne goes way over the top on this lighter-waving tearjerker from the Jim Steinman school of over-production. After a weepy violin intro played by someone anonymous, we get tender piano and Payne's imitation of singer Michael Bolton, with a hint of Meat Loaf on the side. The pompous production is as you'd expect. Inexplicably, this goes on for six minutes.

Supposedly, the guitar solo is not performed by Pitrelli but by Swedish guitarist Mats Johanson, uncredited. It would appear to be Carl Palmer on drums – and does sound like his style on some of the ELP ballads of the 1990s – but it may be Glockler or Sturgis. Again, there is no personality injected, so it could be anyone. This was never played live. Payne gives his all vocally on this one, but the song is just too slick, clichéd and overwrought for listening pleasure, sounding nothing at all like Asia. Ironically, something like this might have hit it big in 1986, but not in 1992.

'A Far Cry' (Downes/Hart/Mitchell/Payne)

Here is a song that at least tries to contain elements of the past Asia sound here and there. It isn't overly-original, but the chorus has some good hooks if slightly marred by Payne's vocal histrionics that do become overwhelming. John would become a much better singer on future Asia albums and wouldn't need to prove himself as much as he does here. He is just trying too hard to inject his personality into the song.

There are keyboards from Downes that add grandiosity, Pitrelli has guitar parts that beef things up, and Howe plays a supple acoustic solo in the middle section. It turns out to be a pretty good listen after a while, but certain elements are too generic at times.

Starting off in the tour setlist, 'A Far Cry' was eventually dropped.

'Don't Call Me' (Downes/Warman)

This is a cover of a little-known song by British singer/songwriter Johnny Warman, who would also co-write several other songs on *Aqua*. The original is typical mid-1980s pop, but Asia's treatment is darker and has some eerie keyboard squelches along with a (mostly) restrained vocal by Payne.

The guitars are low in the mix and the solo is mysterious and effective. The drums are blasé and could be Sturgis or Glockler, or perhaps even programmed. The fairly decent lyrics are about betrayal, deceit and empty promises. The chorus is a little pedestrian, lyrically, but works in this context of anger and resentment, and the chord choices are quite nice.

The song's opening has a phone call being placed amidst some background noise (an airport perhaps?), and if you listen very carefully with the sound turned way up, it sure sounds like 'Heat Of The Moment' is being played through the phone digits being dialled. Very clever and amusing, dare I say. 'Don't Call Me', surprisingly, appeared on the *Silent Nation* tour in 2005 and sounded pretty good when stripped down.

'Heaven On Earth' (Nye/Payne)

We're now back to power ballad city with 'Heaven On Earth'. While this track shares the weaker qualities of some of the album's songs, there are some saving graces. Payne overdoes it vocally, no doubt about that, but he also displays his unquestionable singing talents.

The song is darkly-shaded, with chilling keyboards in the intro, first verse and chorus. The listener can tell it's building to something big. It's not until the 1:30 mark where the guitars and drums come in, and by the second chorus, it's sound is bombastic.

Yes, the backing vocals are overdone again, and Payne's enunciation on certain lyrics is annoying (the 'sweetest poison, positive attraction' line is not particularly good), but there's something about this track that is very well done. There are nuances here that are quite effective. Around the three-minute mark, the song goes totally dark with haunting keyboards, the occasional ghostly guitar screech, and cymbals and bass effects before Carl Palmer hits a booming fill at 3:41, leading to an absolutely crushing solo by Pitrelli.

Asia never played the song live, though Payne did do a solo acoustic version on some TV appearances to promote the album. It was issued as a single but went nowhere.

'Aqua Part 2' (Downes/Payne)

And thus *Aqua* ends as it began, with an instrumental piece. This track – all Downes' work – is ambient keyboard washes and more aquatic sounds, with some programming and symphonic keyboard stabs. If only the rest of *Aqua* had been as progressive as the beginning and ending, we'd have had a very different album.

It's the hair-metal qualities of certain tracks, the big power ballads and the Frankenstein-like patching together of the 1988-1991 songs and demos that stops the album from having an unique identity, sound or direction. Payne tried too hard to put his own stamp on things. But there really are some very good songs here, and Rodney Matthews created an awesome cover design (the US release had a slightly different cover which looked better). If Howe and Palmer were actually on the whole album, things would have been much different. For what it is, though, *Aqua* has enough to swim through and enjoy. Just be wary of some very fishy moments.

Aqua Rarities
'Obsession' (Payne/Rodford)

Another song with over-cooked backing vocals in the chorus, and anonymous, slick riffs. 'Obsession' is a true B-side. It's second rate material, especially lyrically. There is some quality lead guitar work here (by either Pitrelli or Ant Glynne), but that's all there is to recommend this one. Glockler plays the drums on this cut, but it really sounds like what it is: Downes with Payne and some session men. This was used as a B-side in some territories and was a bonus track on the 2004 *Aqua* remaster.

'Heart Of Gold' (Downes/Payne)

There needs to be an explanation for how this song didn't make the album, while material such as 'Crime Of The Heart', 'Little Rich Boy' and 'Someday', did. 'Heart Of Gold' has a lot of good qualities and was one of the first songs that Downes and Payne wrote together. It was intended for inclusion on *Aqua*, but somehow missed the cut.

The song opens with sweet guitar harmonies, slowly building to the first verse. The chord choices are dramatic and appropriate, and the chorus is anthemic without being too over the top. As usual, there are loads of vocals on the chorus, but it's not as overcooked as a lot of the album's other tracks.

The guitar solo is really well played and leads to a rare keyboard solo where Downes doesn't utilise the symphonic blasts. The structure and arrangement are very radio-friendly and this should've been on the album proper. It was used as a B-side to 'Who Will Stop The Rain?' in the US.

'I Can't Wait A Lifetime' (Nye/Payne)

This track was also considered for the album but didn't make it. It was written by Payne and Andy Nye (ex-Michael Schenker Group) back in 1989 and is a demo recording that ended up on the 1996 rarities compilation, *Archiva 1*. It's clearly not fully-developed and is just another power ballad, but not without some potential.

'Fight Against The Tide' (Nye/Payne)

Here's another one that could have improved *Aqua* by 20,000 leagues. The song has all kinds of things going on, including an a capella opening that sounds inspired by Queen. The verses have some Beatles/ELO influence in the chords, and then there's a flashy guitar/keyboard romp that comes out of nowhere and sounds like Yes.

Real drums hadn't been added yet, but this song screamed potential. It sounds very much like Payne on lead guitar, and he acquits himself well with some nice note-bending, though the tone is too thin. At least this track was included on *Archiva 1* so fans could hear it. A missed opportunity.

Aria (1994)

Personnel:
John Payne: bass, vocals, guitars
Al Pitrelli: guitars
Geoff Downes: keyboards
Michael Sturgis: drums
Released: 31 May 1994 (UK, Japan, Europe), 15 May 1995 (US)
Recorded: Parkgate (Sussex, UK) and Mason Rogue (London, UK) November
1993-March 1994
Producers: Geoff Downes, John Payne
Engineer: Andy Reilly
Cover Illustration: Roger Dean
Highest Chart Position: Japan: 20, Germany: 89, Switzerland: 31

Asia returned in 1994 with an album few could find or even knew existed.
Such was life for many veteran rock acts in the mid-1990s. Shaky management
plagued the band, and they had to scramble for independent deals all over
the world. The album wouldn't even see a proper US release until a full year
after the European one.

Aria was a better album than *Aqua,* as this time around, it was an actual
band making the album, and no session men, guests or additional writers.
Asia were hopelessly unaware of the times musically, and perhaps that's
best: would a listener really want Asia to go grunge? That being said, there
was no chance music like this would sell in 1994. And sell it did not,
unfortunately.

'Anytime' (Downes/Payne)

Aria opens with the immaculately-produced pop confection, 'Anytime'. This
song is pure AOR, but it's clean, crisp and rich in detail: a testament to the
quality attention given to both the production and songwriting craft.

The hi-hat sounds ultra-clean, as does the snare, and drummer Michael
Sturgis plays with both finesse and dignity at once. Al Pitrelli's guitars chime
and every last note is heard, while Geoff Downes adds his mix of organ and
synth touches. John Payne sings with confidence and panache, clearly putting
his imprint on the band's own music now, rather than chasing other styles.
Thankfully, the huge layers of choruses are scaled back (to some degree) on
Aria, which allows the songs to breathe and cut through.

'Anytime' opens with a minute of keyboard ambience, till the guitars chime
and the song begins. The drumming and John Payne's vocals are what really
stand out. Maybe ten years earlier it would've been a hit, but in 1994 it stood
no chance. Payne's fine bass work is also heard far more prominently in the
mix than on *Aqua.*

'Anytime' was played live on the brief *Aria* tour but would not be performed
by Asia again. A music video created for the song was barely shown anywhere.

'Are You Big Enough?' (Downes/Payne)

This unwelcome return to the poor spots of *Aqua* was, thankfully, just a brief diversion. The song begins with a big vocal-only chorus and some weak keyboard sounds that sound very dated for 1994. It's just more lukewarm pop-metal and a definite album sore spot. That being said, with musicians this good at its core, the music itself isn't so bad.

'Are You Big Enough?' was played on the 1994 dates, but not beyond. It actually translated mildly better in a live setting but was not a worthy choice for any setlist.

'Desire' (Downes/Nye/Payne)

'Desire' is an intriguing song with some unusual stylings for the band. It slinks along with a sultry feel and sees Payne in fine form, throwing in some interesting fretless bass. The verses are snaky, building tension into the choruses, which become electric. Downes sweetens the track with keyboard runs at the end.

While the lyrics aren't the best and there are still some weak moments, overall, this track works pretty well. 'Desire' proved to be a good live number on this tour but did not last beyond that.

'Summer' (Downes/Payne)

A more mellow side is shown in 'Summer'. It's an acoustic-based mid-tempo number allowing Payne's commanding vocals to really shine. However, the production is a little too busy and geared towards the adult contemporary crowd, but that's to be expected with a song of this nature.

Things pick up around the 2:45 mark when Pitrelli delivers an emotive solo. There's also a lot of backing vocals here, but at least they are lower in the mix. 'Summer' was usually played acoustically in concert and sounded rather good.

'Sad Situation' (Downes/Payne)

A dramatic weeper, 'Sad Situation' shows Payne in excellent standing vocally and not overdoing things at all. The music is sorrowful, and Pitrelli captures that with his tasteful solos. Downes' keyboard textures accent the verses, and Payne reaches an extremely high range on the pre-choruses. The choruses are on the money, with Payne throwing in some great inflexions.

Sturgis changes the feel by switching from hi-hat to ride cymbal in the closing choruses. The song ends abruptly, and as one would suspect, so does the relationship being detailed. There's even an echo of late-1970s Doobie Brothers on this track, which you could easily hear Michael McDonald lending his soulful talents to.

The song was performed live, both in a full-band arrangement, and later, acoustically stripped-down. It sounded strong either way, which is a credit to how well-written the song was.

'Don't Cut The Wire (Brother)' (Downes/Payne)

One of the better cuts on the album, 'Don't Cut The Wire', seems to tell the tale of two brothers on opposite sides of the tracks, with one making some poor choices. The phased keyboard sounds are pretty cool and the song is the first on the album to rock out.

Though the verses are decidedly dour, the breakdowns before the chorus are pretty heavy and come solo time, Pitrelli gets to lay down some scorching leads utilising slide guitar. The pre-solo breakdown has Sturgis aping Palmer's military snare rolls before the song kicks into higher gear with blazing leads and powerful drumming.

It's nice hearing Pitrelli play like this – but just as he really starts to shred, the song fades! This is not the only time this happens on the album. Although this song wasn't played live beyond the *Aria* tour, it was a lively concert choice.

'Feels Like Love' (Downes/Payne)

The minor opening chords here lead to a set of verses that do tend to drag a little. But then, in sweeps, an utterly tranquil piano melody with a few faint keyboard touches. John Payne harmonises with himself, and the guitars and drums come crashing in for a stellar chorus, taking the song to another level.

The bridge takes on a spiritual feel, Pitrelli adds a solo, and we are back to the piano melody, now played on organ. Payne simply blasts out the repeating refrain, 'It feels like love', almost like a gospel number. Sturgis' pummeling drums follow, taking the song through the repeating full-instrumentation chorus to the finale.

As it turns out, 'Feels Like Love' is a quality song. Payne should be rightfully proud of his performance here. *Aria* is truly where he came into his own, not only as a singer but as the frontman of Asia or at least what was called Asia. This song exemplifies the high quality of the Payne-era, even if it wasn't necessarily Asia. This was another song that was usually performed acoustically live and quite effectively.

'Remembrance Day' (Downes/Payne)

This war-themed track is certainly the heaviest on the album. The riffs are borderline metal, and the choruses are back to those big, anthemic chants that marred many of the songs on *Aqua*. However, the song has such grandeur and power that it seems appropriate this time around. Payne doesn't resort to the vocal shenanigans of *Aqua* here, instead trusting himself and the song to carry the day.

The verses are the opposite of the metallic riffs, easing off into a melodic peace that eventually gives way to the big choruses. Into the chorus, Downes' trumpet-like synths are mixed low but add a regal feel, while Sturgis plays his drums with precision. The song moves by way too quickly, almost as if they thought it was somehow too long (it's barely over four minutes). As Pitrelli starts to crank out what you feel will be a climactic guitar solo, the fade – bizarrely – comes in immediately, almost as if someone fell asleep at the mixing desk and their beer spilt on the faders. What they were thinking, who knows. On top of that, as Pitrelli starts to unleash his flurry of notes, Sturgis pounds the drums in double time, going for broke. Sadly, you can barely hear any of this taking place. The fade really tarnishes a track that could've been extended to its benefit. At least in concert, the song did take off much more and allowed the musicians to do their thing.

'Enough's Enough' (Downes/Payne)
This song starts out fairly downbeat and never really gets going. Payne hits some falsetto notes and sings extremely well, but it's pretty much standard AOR that goes nowhere special.

The chorus is too large, with a gospel choir in the background and silly handclaps that are distracting. While definitely not a poor song by any means, 'Enough's Enough' is not a very strong song. Downes has a synth solo, but it seems a tad out of place. The key change at the end, and the enormous amount of voices, are also a bit too emphatic. The song does showcase John Payne's tremendous vocal pipes and that's not an entirely bad thing here.

'Military Man' (Downes/Payne)
Perhaps the best-loved track on *Aria* – amongst the fanbase of the Payne years – 'Military Man' really ups the ante musically and lyrically. This was a song idea the guys had kicking around during the sessions for *Aqua*, but they ran out of time and didn't want to rush it. This turned out to be a good thing, as they clearly dedicated time to get it right in the end.

A heavy opening with block power chords and a classic keyboard sound from Downes is followed by Pitrelli's searing guitars. Sturgis then lends a drum shuffle for the verse, continuing through the excellent chorus.

The chorus has some of the album's finest lyrics:

So don't come running here to find me
'Cause I'm a military man
And as I spin this wheel of fortune
In my military world
I'm a military man

The bridge has some lovely keyboard parts, and Pitrelli's outro solo absolutely cooks. When Guthrie Govan took over on guitar, he energised the song even further when it was performed in concert. 'Military Man' was definitely a great vehicle for the live setting, and the song remained in the live set for the rest of the Payne era.

'Aria' (Downes/Nye/Payne)
The album concludes with this short but effective piece, which is only Downes on piano/keyboards, and Payne on vocals. The opening chords echo Paul

McCartney's writing, and Payne sings with reserve. The sparse arrangement is haunting, particularly when Downes' synth refrain from 'Desire' resurfaces, then fades back down to solely the piano again.

Conclusion

Such a dramatic yet brief conclusion is fitting, as the album certainly went through different moods and parts of life lyrically. Not everything was good, but the majority of the album was well done, and at least it established that Geoff and John could not only still write some good songs but could also do a good job on the production end.

Despite it being a pretty good album, music that was out of touch with 1994 meant dismal sales. But the guys would keep at it, with more music in them still to go. The band tried to tour the album in the summer and fall of 1994, but management barely scheduled any dates with promoters, and in some of the few cities they did play, there was no promotion whatsoever. After playing only a few scattered dates, Pitrelli left, joining prog-metal act Savatage and later, Megadeth. (Later, the Christmas act, Trans-Siberian Orchestra – now a worldwide sensation – requested Pitrelli's services, and he is still with them to this day). Former Simply Red guitarist, Aziz Ibrahim, took Pitrelli's place in Asia, and though there were still long gaps between dates, a decent amount of shows took place in Europe (mostly in Germany) and in Japan.

It became quite clear that if the Asia name was to survive, Downes and Payne would have to keep expectations and costs down and expect to struggle.

Aria Rarities
'Reality' (Downes/Payne)

'Reality' is actually a fun song and very worthy of album inclusion. The problem was, that sounding like nothing else on the album, it didn't fit, so was banished to B-side status. It's a quirky new wave/pop tune with squeaky synths and even some wonderfully cheesy voice synthesizer on the chorus.

Thomas Dolby, Ultravox and even The Buggles have a hand in influencing this song. Al Pitrelli's solo is simple and perfect for the song, and Geoff Downes has equally simple fills towards the conclusion. 'Reality' is a nifty little pop tune, firmly rooted in 1980 or so. What's wrong with that? Nothing! This was included on *Archiva 2* and as a bonus track on the remaster.

Arena (1996)

Personnel:
John Payne: bass, guitars, vocals
Aziz Ibrahim: guitars
Elliot Randall: guitars
Geoff Downes: keyboards
Michael Sturgis: drums
Additional musicians: Hotei Tomoyasu (guitar on 'Into The Arena'), Luis Jardim (percussion)
Released: 17 February 1996 (Japan), 4 March 1996 (UK and Europe)
Recorded: Electric Palace (London, UK) June-December 1995
Producers: Geoff Downes, John Payne
Engineers: John Brough, John Payne
Cover Illustration: Rodney Matthews
Highest Chart Positions: Japan: 48, Switzerland: 50

In 1996, Asia released their sixth studio album, *Arena*. This new album was the most consistent of the John Payne era so far and saw the group returning to their progressive rock roots, as well as trying elements of other musical styles, including jazz, Latin, reggae, progressive metal and Middle Eastern music.

Arena was diverse and was one of the band's more enjoyable efforts. By this point, John Payne had become a really solid vocalist, writer and producer. Once again, this was a band effort, with Aziz Ibrahim on guitar (he had replaced Pitrelli during the fractured *Aria* tour) and new recruit Elliot Randall (ex-Steely Dan), who gave the band a jazzier feel.

Sadly, the album did not get a US release, which was a real shame, and the UK release was largely a secret. With no US deal, the band decided that there would be no tour for the album either.

It's hard to believe *Arena* is over 20 years old, but indeed it is. It featured an amazing cover illustration from Rodney Matthews: still a work of art to marvel at all these years later. Downes and Payne may have been struggling to get any recognition for their work at this point, but this was an album to be proud of. It's really only in the last few years that the Payne era has received some much-deserved attention.

'Into The Arena' (Downes/Payne/Randall/Tomoyasu)
Perhaps sliding a little too close to cocktail jazz, 'Into The Arena' is an instrumental that features Japanese guitar legend Hotei, and percussionist, Luis Jardim. There's a touch of Santana to the track, but it's all a little too clean, polite and sterile. One might even hear this at a dentist's office or in the supermarket.

The playing is tasteful and delicate but is background music and nothing more. Hotei is a guitar god, though, and getting him on a track was wonderful. Elliott Randall also adds some jazz guitar touches and plays fluently.

'Arena' (Downes/Payne)

From 'Into The Arena' to 'Arena' we go. This song stays at a mellow jazz pace, with even a touch of R&B in the mix. Again, it's extremely delicate but not overly slick. Payne sounds great singing in a lower register, and there's a killer guitar solo from Randall.

'Arena' has such a late-1970s smoothness to it that comparisons to Ambrosia (they did start as a prog-rock band after all), Player and Alan Parsons Project, are not without merit. It was one of the few *Arena* songs to be played live, and when Guthrie Govan ripped into the solo on this one in concert, let's just say it was divine.

'Heaven' (Downes/Payne)

This beautiful pop confection is a Downes/Payne gem. The opening guitar motif is a choppy staccato riff with a lot of delay on it. Faint keyboards accompany it, giving off a huge Pink Floyd vibe (think 'Another Brick In The Wall (Part 2)' meets 'Run Like Hell' meets 'Keep Talking' meets 'Take It Back'). The melodies and hooks are stupendous, and Payne does a wonderful job on the lead guitar solo, even throwing in harmonies at the end.

After the solo and some wah-wah guitar, Downes adds perfectly-placed synth strings, Sturgis builds the chorus up with expert drumming, and the song continues to soar to the heavens. Geoff closes the song with a sweet dose of synths and electric piano, as Payne joins him singing a wispy vocal until the song's last note.

The Payne years really gave us some quality music, and I would choose this song as an example to prove that John Payne is a gifted musician. In a perfect world, 'Heaven' would've been a monster hit. But alas, only the faithful knew of it.

'Two Sides Of The Moon' (Downes/Payne)

Here's a different one, to say the least. 'Two Sides Of The Moon' has a vaguely Japanese feel, and opens with a guitar line that's pretty much a dead ringer for Van Stephenson's cornball 1984 hit, 'Modern Day Delilah'.

The song deals with two people connecting from different backgrounds. At least that's what I think it's about. The lyrics – like many on this album – are a little obtuse and don't make a whole lot of sense. Or maybe they do; what do I know? Lines such as, 'Data streaming through my window, Chrome stars whispering their lies, Black sky hides approaching danger, Reach out, Two should now be as one', are a little on the pretentious side and make sense perhaps only to John Payne.

It's a melodic song with nice chord changes and an ethereal-sounding chorus. It's the mid-section where, out of nowhere, a Latin rock break occurs, with heavy power chords, flailing percussion, and a Randall guitar solo that any Steely Dan fan would love. It's the ending where things go awry: an ill-advised stab at reggae seems to be there just for being-there's sake. Otherwise, this is a pretty good song and well worth hearing.

'The Day Before The War' (Downes/Payne)

By far the longest Asia song to date, 'The Day Before The War' is a full-on progressive metal epic. Running at just over nine minutes long, the song goes through a variety of changes. A lot of open spaces set up the menacing eruption of the final two minutes, which takes the band into Dream Theater territory. Ibrahim plays a solo utilizing speedy hammer-ons, pull-offs and tremolo bar, while Sturgis drums with fiery precision and counters the choppy guitar bursts as the song fades.

Downes plays eerie synthesizer licks throughout, and Payne plays chilling acoustic guitar. The song has more spacious, quiet parts than explosive ones, but it can't all be bombastic. The thunderous opening segment with double-kick drums and pummeling organ, echoes Yes at their heaviest (i.e. 'Machine Messiah'). What a treat it would've been to hear this song in concert. But with no tour for the album, it never happened, even in later tours.

'The Day Before The War' is proof positive that Asia still had a love for progressive music. With musicians on board with the chops to pull it off, the result is pretty impressive, though the length of the track isn't quite justified, as there are too many mellow parts where things tend to drag. Still, this track does pack a wallop at times and is intriguing, especially with its chilling sci-fi feel.

'Never' (Downes/Payne)

The opening synth fill sounds a little dated for the late 1990s, but 'Never' is a pleasant enough pop song. Subtle guitar parts from Ibrahim, and little interconnecting guitar/keyboard hooks during the pre-choruses, are lovely ear candy. Downes' piano is quite nice during the verse before giving way to the synths. He uses organ during the choruses, and there's a funky little guitar part going on as well.

This track sounds like a cross between Toto and Survivor, and easily could've connected at Adult Contemporary radio. A floating synth pattern around 4:00 gives way to a classic Randall solo that instantly sounds like his work with Steely Dan, particularly in the jazz phrasings and picking technique. The song doesn't need to be five and a half minutes long however. Overall, 'Never' proves to be an enjoyable listen and is quite pleasing.

'Falling' (Downes/Payne)

Here we have another pop song with a 1970s keyboard texture in the manner of Supertramp. Payne's vocals reach high, but the song just kind of hangs there, staying in the same motion the whole way through. All the instruments are well mixed, however, and the song is somewhat catchy.

Ibrahim plays the guitars, but he doesn't have much to do here, while Sturgis' drums are snappy and tight. The song has some things going for it but feels more like a B-side than anything else. Geoff's keyboard riff seemed to resurface on 'I Know How You Feel' from the *XXX* album, though within a much better song.

'Words' (Downes/Payne)

Featuring warm acoustic strumming and a sincere lyric, 'Words' is a really good love song. Payne sings with complete conviction, and the musical accompaniment is realised concisely and without too much fuss.

The song begins with heavy, crashing guitars and drums, and the pretty acoustic strumming (by Ibrahim) and soothing synthesizer wash lead to Payne's opening lines. The lead guitar lines – played by Payne – follow the vocal melody.

Though there aren't many lyrics, the ones that are there are poignant:

If I whispered words, would you hear them now?
Would you cross the deepest seas?
In the fiercest winds
On the burning trail
Seal it with your word

These lines repeat a few times, but it works to keep the sentiment sincere and the lyrics sparse.

Payne takes a melodic lead guitar solo, and then come the big, shouty choruses like those so prevalent on *Aqua* and lesser so on *Aria*. In an interview at the time, Downes said to Dave Gallant, 'We wanted to get away from the AOR chorus thing; a big block of voices on every chorus. We still got it to a degree on 'Words' and 'Heaven'. We wanted to get more of an eclectic, players type of album out rather than an AOR sound'.

'Words' definitely has some of that, but not too much, thankfully. It's definitely true that they mostly avoided that direction, and it was a welcome change. Once again, some editing could've helped here as the last minute of the song feels like too much, and at 5:19, the song stays a bit longer than required.

'U Bring Me Down' (Downes/Ibrahim/Payne)

Opening with an Indian-flavoured Led Zeppelin sequence, giving way to a Deep Purple-styled organ-heavy rocker, 'U Bring Me Down' sees the band wearing all kinds of musical hats (don't worry, Payne didn't find his beloved top hat), and creating a quality seven-minute epic.

The choruses are mystical-sounding and have a trance-like feel. Sturgis hits hard, like John Bonham, although the bass drum lacks punch. There is something of a rap in the mid-section which isn't as inappropriate as it sounds, though it definitely was not a good idea.

Around the 4:45 mark, Ibrahim goes for broke with all kinds of serpentine Middle Eastern riffs and solos on electric and acoustic guitars. Right afterwards, Downes laces a wicked synth solo for good measure. The rest of the song has layers of backing vocals, pounding drums, and Ibrahim's snarling leads with a countermelody, though that annoying rap goes throughout the fade. Ibrahim's leads during the lengthy fade are too buried in the mix, though there is a ton going on in this is a progressive and unique track.

The band earn major points for even attempting something like this. Ibrahim specially, really owns this, and his co-writing credit proves it.

'Tell Me Why' (Downes/Payne)

With an opening sounding like a Gary Wright song, 'Tell Me Why' is an acoustic-based ballad with slight keyboard touches from Downes and loads of vocals from Payne. This one might've fit better on the previous album, but it's worthy: largely for Payne's vocals and the mood the track creates.

Randall and Payne handle the guitars (you can definitely tell the difference as to who is who), the outro section showing some nice soloing while Sturgis keeps a steady beat. Downes lays in the background, and like most of the *Arena* tracks, you can barely hear Payne's bass-playing. A fairly nondescript song, 'Tell Me Why' is simple but effective pop.

'Turn It Around' (Downes/Payne/Sturgis)

Another laid-back easy-listening song, 'Turn it Around' has this nagging hook that gets in the listener's ear right away. It's a simple little keyboard fill, but a very strong one. The song stays at the same tempo throughout, not really doing a whole lot, but it doesn't need to.

Released as a single, could this have been a hit at adult contemporary radio? Yes. Although it shares similarities with *Arena*'s few weak cuts, 'Turn It Around' grows on you, it's good qualities becoming obvious after a few listens. Drummer Sturgis gets a co-writing credit here, perhaps for helping with the arrangement.

'Bella Nova' (Downes/Payne)

This essentially solo Geoff Downes outing is an uplifting, beautiful piece of music. The keyboards are bright as a glorious new sun rising or a tranquil snowfall. There are hope, optimism and rejoicing in this piece and all conflict has been resolved. Geoff has always been a master at knowing when not to play, playing with class, and not being too fussy. His impeccable taste is on clear display here.

'Bella Nova' is a wonderful way to wrap up the album, and it ends on a note of such hope, as the lion on the cover has ensured peace will reign. Alas, *Arena* went nowhere fast, and the band couldn't tour due to financial woes. It would be a long time before we heard from the guys again, either in the studio or in concert.

Arena Rarities
'That Season' (Downes/Payne)

It's quite the head-scratcher why this gem didn't make it onto *Arena*. 'That Season' is a lovely song with such a great vibe about it that for it to be relegated

Right: The four original members of Asia in an early promo shot just before they conquered the rock world.

Left: John Payne, the bassist/guitarist/vocalist who kept the Asia flame burning as the front man for fifteen years.

Below: The revamped 2019 Asia lineup including three Yes members along with new front man Ron Thal (ex-Guns 'N' Roses).

Special GUEST APPEARANCE by STEVE HOWE

BILLY SHERWOOD   GEOFF DOWNES   CARL PALMER   RON BUMBLEFOOT THAL

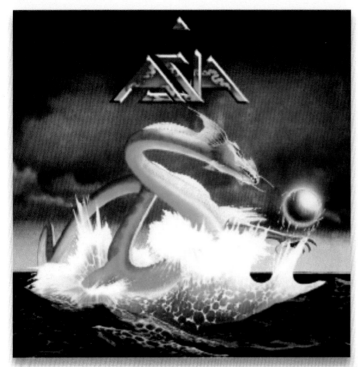

Left: *Asia* – the album that launched the band to massive success, particularly in the USA where it stayed at the number one slot for nine weeks. It has an iconic cover by Roger Dean. (*Geffen Records*)

Right: *Alpha*, the platinum-selling sophomore album released in the summer of 1983 with one of Roger Dean's best designs. (*Geffen Records*)

Right: Roger Dean's futuristic design of a fallen angel named Aza made for a stunning cover for 1985's *Astra* album. (*Geffen Records*)

Left: The Rodney Matthews cover for 1992's *Aqua* album was the first not to be designed by Roger Dean for Asia. This version is signed to the author by Geoff Downes. (*Music For Nations Records/Author Collection*)

Left: 1982's 'Heat of the Moment' would become one of the most played videos in MTV's history and was directed by Godley & Crème. (*Geffen Records*)

Right: Asia with Greg Lake from the infamous 1983 *Asia In Asia* concert aired live to a satellite audience of over 20 million on MTV. (*Vestron Video*)

Left: A clip of new recruit Mandy Meyer from the MTV hit video for 'Go' in 1985 directed by Peter Chistopherson. (*Geffen Records*)

Right: The 1990 reunited lineup with Wetton, Downes, Palmer and new guitarist Pat Thrall on British television. (*Rhino Records*)

Left: John Payne in 2002 when Asia hit the road and toured for the first time since 1994.

Right: Guitarist extraordinaire Guthrie Govan on stage with Asia in 2002. Guthrie is now renowned as one of the true guitar greats.

Left: *Aria* from 1994. A full-band album that contains the Payne era classic 'Military Man'. (*Bullet Proof / Mayhem*)

Right: 1996's *Arena* was the band's most progressive album in years and Rodney Matthews added a stellar cover illustration. (*Resurgence Records*)

Right: *Aura* from 2001 was the the band's first album in five years. Unusually, it featured an outside producer in Simon Hanhart. (*Resurgence Records*)

Left: *Silent Nation* in 2004 was the band's only album for InsideOut and the last album of the John Payne era. (*InsideOut*)

Left: Carl Palmer continues to defy age and time and is still at the top of his game at the age of 70. *(Eagle Records)*

Below: The reunited original Asia lineup in 2007 for the filming of the *Fantasia* live video release. (*Eagle Records*)

Left: Guitarist Steve Howe on stage in Tokyo in 2007 with Carl Palmer drumming behind him. (*Eagle Records*)

Right: The band's reunion tour in 2006-07 was such a success that they stayed together longer this time around than in their glory days. (*Eagle Records*)

Above: Geoff Downes and his wall of keyboards play as integral a role in Asia's music as any other instrument in the band. (*Frontiers Records*)

Right: Young guitarist Sam Coulson on stage in 2013 with Asia. Coulson was recommended to the band by Paul Gilbert of Mr. Big. (*Frontiers Records*)

Left: The appropriately-named *Phoenix* showed that the newly-reformed original line up had lost none of its desire to make new music. (*Frontiers Records*)

Right: *Omega* was a strong follow up to *Phoenix*, and the live shows that surrounded its release were some of the best the band had played. (*Frontiers Records*)

Right: *XXX* was the final album from the band's original line up, and they really made it count! (*Frontiers Records*)

Left: In 2014, Asia issued their final studio album *Gravitas*. The final song 'Till We Meet Again' was an appropriate farewell. (*Frontiers Records*)

Left: 1982's debut single and monster hit 'Heat of the Moment peaked at number 4 on the US Hot 100 Singles. (*Geffen Records/ Author's Collection*)

Right: 'Don't Cry' was another US top ten single and made the top 40 in the UK in the summer of 1983. (*Geffen Records/Author's Collection*)

Left: In 1985, 'Go' was the first single from *Astra* and showed a harder-edged sound with new guitarist Mandy Meyer. (*Geffen Records/Author's Collection*)

Right: In 1990, Asia reformed with a best-of album that featured four new songs titled *Then & Now*. It went gold in America. (*Geffen Records*)

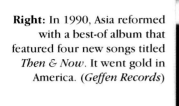

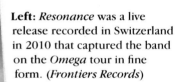

Left: *Resonance* was a live release recorded in Switzerland in 2010 that captured the band on the *Omega* tour in fine form. (*Frontiers Records*)

Right: The 2012 tour was the final one with the original lineup and *Axis XXX Live* was a fantastic finale. (*Frontiers Records*)

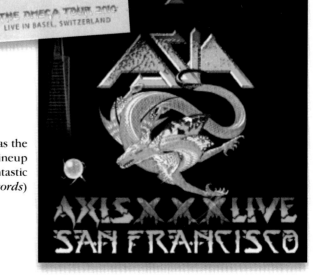

Left: Carl Palmer's fun but unsuccessful foray into new wave music with PM was the album *1:PM* in 1980. (*Manticore Records*)

Right: A promo shot of the band 3 which featured Carl Palmer, Keith Emerson and Robert Berry in 1988. (*Geffen Records*)

Left: The self-titled GTR debut fell just shy of the US top ten and featured two Steves - Hackett and Howe. (*Arista Records*)

Right: Asia's humour shows with the 'Heat of the Moment' oven mitt, which the author has used at a dinner or two. (*Author's Collection*)

Above: Roger Dean returned to design 2001's Aura, here signed by all the band members at the time of release. (*Recognition Records/Author's Collection*)

Right: The author bumped into Carl Palmer at a Yes show in 2013 and he was kind enough to pose in the 'heat of the moment.' (*Author's Collection*)

Above: Asia with the 2019 lineup on their first tour in 2019 with Ron Thal handling vocals and Steve Howe guesting.

Right: Another concert shot of Ron Thal fronting Asia on the 2019 tour with Geoff Downes as always, on keyboards.

Left: The 2019 tour with Billy Sherwood on bass as the band perform the classic 'Only Time Will Tell.'

to a B-side seems criminal. At least the song found a home on the remastered *Arena* in 2005. Payne does some of his finest singing here: so much better than on tracks like 'Falling' or 'Tell Me Why.' Downes sprinkles keyboard parts for colour, and Randall plays tastefully.

'Ginger' (Downes/Howe/Payne)
Having recently reunited with Yes, Steve Howe was busy and failed to submit this acoustic piece in time for it to be included on *Arena*. As always, you can tell it's Steve right off the bat due to his infamous picking style. It's not as memorable (or as good) as 'Aqua Part 1', but it still would've been a better album intro than 'Into The Arena'. It's nice to see it find a home on *Archiva 1*.

'Don't Come To Me' (Schwartz)
This was considered for the album was never properly finished. 'Don't Come To Me' was written by Canadian songwriter, Eddie Schwartz, who wrote smash hits like 'Hit Me With Your Best Shot' by Pat Benatar and 'Don't Shed A Tear' by Paul Carrack. It's a moody, downbeat track, and not without some charm. It ended up on *Archiva 2*.

'We Fall Apart' (Downes/Payne)
One of the first tracks written for *Arena*, this one missed the cut, allegedly because the guys felt it was too industrial-sounding. But that can't be the reason, because we're not exactly talking Ministry or Skinny Puppy here. Most likely, it didn't make the album because it was a little different and maybe a touch too electropop – but industrial it most certainly is not. It's a pretty decent song, though, with slight shades of Duran Duran and David Bowie if you listen hard enough. A home would be found for this on *Archiva 1*.

'The Smoke That Thunders' (Downes/Palmer/Payne)
Here was another desperate attempt to get an original band member on *Arena*. Carl Palmer's drums from *Aqua*'s 'The Voice Of Reason' were sampled and used here, and Downes added some ELP-sounding synths and keyboard styles. It's not really a song this one: just some ideas that sound like a demo over the top of drums that had been recorded years prior. *Archiva 2* is where it ended up.

'Showdown' (Lynne)
This cover of the 1973 ELO classic shows Payne in fine form. John was briefly in ELO Part II, but around 1990, left the project after several months. That was a shame for him, as ELO Part II did quite well, touring for a decade.

This recording is nothing more than a demo with bad drum programming and lousy sounding guitars, but it was considered for inclusion on *Arena*. This recording would appear on *Archiva 2*.

'Right To Cry' (Downes/Payne)

Another tune from the *Arena* sessions, this ballad would appear on *Archiva 2*, and quite frankly, it's not that good. Clearly a demo, the song is clichéd and dull, with little going for it musically. This is why they're called outtakes. Most of what appears on the *Archiva* compilations should've stayed unreleased, but a few nuggets were enjoyable.

Conclusion

With few sales and no tour, the *Arena* album disappeared, as did the band. In 1997, Downes, Payne, Ibrahim and percussionist Bob Richards did an unplugged show in Germany: the lone Asia concert between 1995 and 2001.

Later in 1997, the band wanted to celebrate their 15th anniversary with a tour behind the compilation, *Anthology: The Best of Asia,* but the album did not get a US release. It featured five forgettable re-recordings of Asia classics from the 1980s: recordings the fans did not enjoy. Nor did John Wetton and John Payne would also acknowledge it wasn't a good idea. There would be no tour. Downes and Payne then did soundtrack work for a Sony PlayStation game and a BBC documentary about salmon. This material would surface on a low-budget compilation titled *Rare*.

In 1999 there were talks to reunite the original lineup, but that idea fell through when Howe was unavailable due to his Yes commitments. David Kilminster (now with Roger Waters) from John Wetton's band, was set to take over, but without Howe's involvement, promoters backed out. Wetton and Palmer then formed Qango, with Kilminster and John Young. Asia eventually got back into the studio again, with a new approach.

Aura (2001)

Personnel:
John Payne: bass, guitars, vocals
Guthrie Govan: guitars
Geoff Downes: keyboards
Chris Slade: drums
Additional musicians: Steve Howe, Elliott Randall, Pat Thrall, Ian Crichton (guitars);
Tony Levin, Gary Leiderman (bass); Simon Phillips, Vinnie Colaiuta, Michael Sturgis
(drums); Luis Jardim (percussion)
Released: 31 January 2001 (Japan), 12 February 2001 (UK and Europe)
Recorded: Studio Loco (Monmouthshire, Wales) January-August 2000
Producers: Simon Hanhart and Asia
Engineer: Simon Hanhart
Cover Illustration: Roger Dean
Highest Chart Position: UK: 160

In 2001, Asia released *Aura*: their first studio album in five years. The guys
spent a long time making it, and as usual there were label troubles: this time
with Recognition Records. This label would get the band no recognition, as it
went under shortly after *Aura* was released, leaving the album to sink without
much of a chance.

This was very unfortunate, as *Aura* was arguably the band's best album of the
John Payne era.

Downes and Payne had finally brought in an outside producer in Simon
Hanhart, whose production credits included Marillion, Saxon, Arena, Tin
Machine and Matthew Sweet. Hanhart was well-renowned for his engineering
and mixing skills, and it's no surprise that *Aura* was also the best album,
sonically, of the Payne era.

The album returned to the committee feel of *Aqua*, but thankfully, this
time around the songs hadn't been culled from various aborted projects.
The material was newly-written and utilised some of the best players in the
business. Former Asia members Howe, Randall, Thrall and Sturgis, would also
play key roles.

Roger Dean designed one of his all-time best artistic visions for the cover.
And with such a solid (and lengthy) album – and an actual tour planned with
a steady, solidified lineup of Downes, Payne, guitar wizard, Guthrie Govan.
and drumming great, Chris Slade – things were looking up. Unfortunately, the
public at large remained hard to convince.

'Awake' (Downes/Payne)
Opening their new album with a soaring, spiritual opus, Asia certainly wanted
the listener's attention, and 'Awake' is a sterling moment in the band's
recording career. The lyrics were adapted from *The Rubiyat of Omar Khayyam:*
a collection of quatrains by the man who was labelled the Astronomer-Poet

of Persia. Edward FitzGerald had translated the work from Persian to English and released it in 1859. It was not a big hit at first but caught on a few years later. It was pretty heady stuff for Asia to be tackling and was definitely within the realm of something a true progressive rock band would attempt, and a successful attempt it was.

As colourful as anything they'd recorded to this point, Asia crafted a winner with 'Awake'. The bubbling keyboard fills percolate alongside choppy guitar parts, and the chord changes exhibit a serious vibrancy that really gets to the human spirit.

The opening lyrics set the tone of the writing theme and song inspiration:

I saw the writing on the wall
The story of our birth and then the fall
Within their tombs of holy stone
The scrolls of life, one man alone
So if we try, we can live and learn
The sand will pull you under
Don't let them pull you under

Downes has a lovely vintage-sounding synth solo, and the choir at the end is vibrant and an inspired choice. Guthrie Govan's guitars are impeccable, fitting the song perfectly, while Michael Sturgis does a wonderful job on drums, adding fills where needed, keeping things lively and bright rhythmically. 'Awake', a fantastic live number, really excelled in a concert setting.

'Wherever You Are' (Downes/Gold/Gouldman/Payne)
A straightforward pop song, 'Wherever You Are' was quite radio-friendly, with excellent keyboard work from Downes and a divine double-tracked guitar solo from Govan. The solo leaps out of nowhere and shows how inventive and skilled Govan is as a player. Payne sings to serve the song, showcasing his maturity as a singer by this point, and Chris Slade's drumming is tight. This song could've easily found its way onto the radio, which seemed to be the goal. But that didn't happen, yet again.

'Wherever You Are' is one of the best pop songs of the Payne era. It had all the right touches and sounded good live, though in concert, it missed the subtle nuances of the studio recording. Andrew Gold (of 'Lonely Boy' fame) and Graham Gouldman (of 10cc) co-wrote this one, and the results were first rate.

'Ready To Go Home' (Gold/Gouldman)
Some songs can stir something in a listener, bringing out a variety of emotions, and 'Ready To Go Home' is certainly one of them. Probably the best-recorded vocal performance of the John Payne years, this track is actually a cover of a little-known 10cc song. Payne delivers a soul-stirring vocal. From the first note,

the song is exquisite, and Payne's opening lines are wonderfully understated. The use of the David Grant Gospel Choir adds even more layers of beauty. The track is perfectly-recorded and mixed, and the playing is supremely executed. Downes plays with delicacy, and Guthrie Govan's guitar solo couldn't be more apt for this type of song. Add two legendary musicians as the rhythm section – bassist Tony Levin and drummer Vinnie Colaiuta – and you've got something special indeed.

There are so many heart-wrenching lyrical passages that it's hard not to quote them all, but some are just astonishing:

Take this river to the sea
Where the delta flows
The tide is washing over me
Guide this soul to Heaven's door
Show me where tomorrow lies
I'm waiting to be born

This sure seems to be about the passing of a life and it is incredibly moving. Other lines also accent this: 'So tired I lay down, With these memories, Breathe shallow deep inside of me, If time has run its course with me'. If that's not moving enough, the elegiac chorus is totally spiritual in both music and verse: 'I'm ready to go home, I'm ready to receive, Forgiveness for my sins, I'm ready to begin'.

Asia knew the importance of this song, and they delivered the goods here in a huge way. The best thing about this recording is that it never approaches bombast or mawkishness and remains tasteful and elegant the whole way through.

Then there's the last verse:

When the evening shadows fall
When the time has come
I'll let defenses fall
To surrender's to survive
I will give up everything
To those I leave behind

This is spiritual and certainly about a peaceful resignation when it is time for any of us to 'go home'. And if there was any doubt, the feeling is in the last chorus: 'I'm ready to lay down, I'm ready now to sleep, A promise I must keep, I'm ready to go home, again'.

More people need to know of this song, whether it's the version by Asia, 10cc, or the amazing vocalist Morten Harket of A-ha. Asia even did a Spanish version, available as a mail-order-only offer. Thankfully, the song was played live on the *Aura* tour.

'The Last Time' (Downes/Payne)

This song is a tasty one. It opens with pulsating synths and drums from Vinnie Colaiuta echoing the style of The Police' Stewart Copeland. Colaiuta's drumming is magnificent, as you get to hear the world-class musician he truly is. The choruses have a certain sultry quality to them. In fact, this song would not be out of place on Sting's excellent 1993 album *Ten Summoner's Tales*. The bridge is beautifully constructed, and vocally, Payne is at the top of his game.

The solo section features Steve Howe doing jazz runs, while Saga's Ian Crichton strikes some wailing leads in contrast. Both Howe and Crichton briefly trade solos in the end section.

I asked Steve Howe in our interview when the album came out about appearing on the album when I interviewed him at the time the album was released:

I like the sense that Asia has gone into quality again. You know, they are trying to get the quality standard of the style of progressive rock, that sort of thing. Some of the things they go into aren't up my street as much as other things, and that's why I was able to play on the two tracks that I felt comfortable with when they were at the stage they were. There is a lot of finish and polish on the record, and I think Geoff's done a good job.

'The Last Time' is another in a long line of this album's great moments.

'Forgive Me' (Downes/Payne/Santis/Tancredi)

This nifty little tune is a pleasant earworm. Downes lays down the foundation with some pumping synth chords, and Sturgis plays an irresistible drum groove throughout with some great hi-hat work again. Payne remains confident and sincere with his vocal approach: not overdoing anything. Govan adds slight textural guitar touches, but there's no solo, which is fine.

You could call this style sophisticated adult contemporary: another song that would have been a nice fit for radio. This song's sound is an example of what Simon Hanhart brought to the table with his mixing and production skills.

'Kings Of The Day' (Downes/Payne)

Coming in at nearly seven minutes, this is a slow-burning progressive number with a slight jazz feel and spacey atmospherics largely supplied by Downes on keyboards. Simon Phillips plays drums and Govan's guitars chime away in the background during the verses.

At times it feels like a cross between The Alan Parsons Project and Steely Dan: Govan's guitar solo definitely showcases a serious Steely Dan vibe. Music like this simply isn't written very often these days.

'Kings of the Day' is lyrically deep and seems sadly prescient for today:

Looking in the distance
The fever on the street
Cast away the covers
Let my people see
Rulers of the network
Leaders from the dark
Embrace a generation
The first will be the last

Having both a progressive and accessible appeal, 'Kings Of The Day' is
an excellent example of how far the John-Payne-era Asia had come – both
musically and lyrically – from the days of 'Back In Town' and 'Little Rich Boy'.

'The Coldest Day In Hell' (Downes/Payne/Woolfenden)

This song is perhaps a little too similar in style to some of the others, and it
definitely goes on far too long at six and a half minutes. But there is still a
reward to be found.

Payne sings this haunting rumination in a classy style, and Downes' keyboard
arsenal really lays on some thick atmospherics. Some of those sounds are quite
vintage: like Wetton-era Asia. There's a bit of a Pink Floyd vibe here, but the
song feels like it extended itself too far and either needed more musical muscle
or a few minutes of editing.

One thing is for sure: this is an involved song. But after a few listens, you
can see what they were going for, even if it seems a tad cluttered and a bit of a
downer.

'Free' (Downes/Payne)

And now we arrive at a seriously intense piece of music with. Any fan of
progressive music should go nuts for this propulsive eight-minute barn burner.

Downes attacks with a vengeance, squelching synths percolating underneath,
while Simon Phillips supplies power and crazed drum fills. The hard-driving
rhythms of the mid-section, set up a wild trio of guitar solos from Howe, Thrall
and Crichton. 'Free' is a genuine Asia classic.

Around the 6:30 mark, the song becomes a gothic piece of Dream Theater-
styled prog-metal, similar to *Arena*'s 'The Day Before The War', only much
more intense. 'Free' is one of the songs from the Payne era that could blow the
mind of a fan doubtful of that part of the band's career; it's that good. An awful
lot of work went into this one, and it was time well spent.

Asia went for a big slice of the progressive rock pie with this epic, and they
delivered in spades. Live, this one was a showcase for Govan's guitar talents.
With a wild solo that drew nightly ovations, he did not disappoint at all.

'You're The Stranger' (Downes/Payne)

This is a pretty straightforward pop song with a light, breezy feel. Sturgis plays the drums, and Randall and Govan are on guitars. Both are fluid and show a Santana-meets-Steely-Dan influence.

'You're The Stranger' has a slightly club-oriented dance feel and is one of a number of tracks that benefit from Luis Jardim's deft percussion touches. Certainly not the best song on the album, it still has nice qualities that make it quite listenable and a fun change-up from the rest of the album. It adds diversity, which is always a good thing, especially on an album this long.

'The Longest Night' (Downes/Payne/Woolfenden)
The problem with 'The Longest Night' is that it's too similar to 'Kings Of The Day' and 'The Coldest Day In Hell'. The basic track moves along at the same sluggish pace and has many of the same atmospherics as the two songs mentioned.

Govan plays a subtle solo with grace and precision, and Colaiuta's drumming is perfect. However, the song never truly gets going and just drags. There's also a depressing feel and a general sense of too much drama that goes nowhere special.

Yet there are still too many qualities to just dismiss this song, and the chorus does feature quality vocals. File this one under decent, but a bit too familiar to other tracks on the record.

'Aura' (Downes/Payne/Randall)
The instrumental track, 'Aura', is a slinky one, with an insistent groove supplied by Randall's funky guitars. Downes adds light synth and piano touches. The rhythm is contagious, with a heavy Latin feel that really comes off well, thanks to Sturgis' creative drumming and Jardim's colourful percussion – his wizardry stealing the show. Randall gives blistering solos, his second leading to the ending, and it is priceless. It's a fantastic way to end an enjoyable album.

The record benefited heavily from the use of an outside producer: one who was also an excellent engineer. No mere filler, 'Aura' – which runs to nearly five minutes – is a piece all of its own and one of the album highlights.

Aura Rarities
'Under The Gun' (Downes/Payne)
One of three bonus tracks on the deluxe version of *Aura*, 'Under The Gun' isn't as menacing as its title. Overall it's a decent mid-tempo pop/rock song, but lacking anything really special, it clearly needed more development. The verses are musically slight, with Downes mixing electric piano and a fat synth lick, the guitars hiding in the background. All three bonus cuts feature what seemed might end up as the new lineup – Crichton on guitar and Slade on drums – but Crichton had to get back to Saga, and Slade fell ill for a while. The ending does feature a touch of talk box guitar but fades out almost immediately.

'Come Make My Day' (Crichton/Downes/Payne)

Opening with strummed acoustic chords and faint keyboards, 'Come Make My Day' is another mid-tempo song that has some seriously questionable lyrics. Among the worst lines are these: 'Another parking fine, Ten more deadly bills, They say it's gonna rain again': not exactly Bob Dylan or Leonard Cohen.

The song is similar to 'Under the Gun' in that it feels underdeveloped, but it has some good portions. Downes has a neat keyboard solo, but confusingly, we hear Crichton start to tear off a guitar solo at the end of the song, right as it fades away, which seems to have become a frustrating tradition in the Payne years. This one wasn't bad at all but needed work. You can tell it was a demo.

'Hands Of Time' (Downes/Payne)

A generic power-chord rocker, this one was easily the weakest of the bonus tracks. The lyrics are sophomoric, and the chorus has too much of the cheesy approach that tainted much of *Aqua*. The sound is also underproduced and clearly of demo quality. The drums and guitars both sound muddled here. This was not up to being considered for inclusion on the album and it's wise they decided not to return to it during the sessions.

Conclusion

In 2001, Asia had a really good album in *Aura* and finally had a tour to embark on. However, Recognition Records went bankrupt, and the album sold poorly. Strangely, Asia went on a co-headlining tour of Europe with former Free, Bad Company and The Firm vocalist Paul Rodgers (my favourite singer). Rodgers is a blues/rock singer with seemingly nothing in common with Asia, so that was odd. Later, they toured with progressive rock legends, Kansas, which made much more sense.

US dates happened later that summer as part of a 1980s package tour with The Fixx, The Outfield and The Motels, but attendance was not stellar. Later in the year, Asia played dates on their own but were relegated to clubs with small audiences.

More European dates took place in 2002, and the band played a solitary US date on 5 October, co-headlining with Uriah Heep, Nektar and Focus, as part of the Classic Rock Festival at the Patriots Theater in Trenton, New Jersey. The show was filmed for a DVD release (which had some issues, sadly) and a double live CD. I was at this show, and it was great to see Asia playing a full set on a big stage. The theatre was only half full, but that did not dampen an outstanding performance.

In 2003, Geoff and John decided to get intimate with the fanbase. They allowed any fan who could provide a stage and $3,000 US to book them for an acoustic gig. Shows took place from Alaska to New Jersey for small, but dedicated gatherings of Asia fans. My pal Dan Fraga booked the guys at the Broadway Theatre in Pitman, NJ. We were their roadies for the day and went out to dinner with them. John and Geoff were great guys, especially John, as we bonded over a plate of gnocchi and a love of cats. The guys played for about an hour and signed autographs for fans. It was an amazing day, and they – and their then-manager Ace Trump – could not have been nicer.

In 2004, it was finally time for another album and the conclusion of the John Payne era.

Silent Nation (2004)

Personnel:
John Payne: bass, guitars, lead vocals
Guthrie Govan: guitars
Geoff Downes: keyboards, percussion
Chris Slade: drums
Additional musicians: Billy Sherwood (guitars, bass), Ant Glynne (guitars), Jay Schellen (drums), Kim Neilsen Parsons (bass)
Released: 31 August 2004
Recorded: Clear Lake Audio (Los Angeles, CA) October 2003-June 2004
Producer: John Payne
Engineer: John Payne
Cover Artwork/Layout: Thomas Ewerhard
Highest chart position: Germany: 77

Silent Nation was to be the final album of the John Payne era, and this time around, Asia went for a dark, brooding, and at times harrowing sound and style. Quite a few of the songs are lengthy, some going on way too long for their own good. Something different about this album is that the guys wrote in the studio, as opposed to just Geoff and John composing songs and bringing in different players at various junctures. Thus, this would be the first 'band' album since *Aria*. It would also be the first Asia studio album not to have a title starting and ending with the letter 'a'.

Payne produced and engineered *Silent Nation*, doing quite the job for the most part. There is a more organic feel sonically, and Geoff Downes uses a lot of organ on the album. But it proved to be the most modern-sounding Asia recording to date, utilising a lot of technology, but to the band's credit, was not fussed up with too much gadgetry.

Silent Nation was still a high-quality album but a comedown from its predecessor. The theme of the average person's world struggles becomes a bit much, making the album a weary listen. But one must applaud the guys for stepping up with something different. Additionally, being on a real label (Inside Out/SPV) was a big reason why everything was so professional.

But yet again, the album did not sell, and the ensuing tour was sparsely attended, to horrid numbers in the US once the tour hit that market in 2005. Shows in the UK and Europe were mildly better. But something had to give for Geoff Downes at this point. He had kept the Asia name alive for years: a tough road to walk. To go from filling 20,000 seat arenas to playing clubs of 100-200 fans was a bitter pill to swallow. It took a while, but something special would be on the way in a couple of years, and it was reconnecting with John Wetton via the iCon project that got the ball rolling.

'What About Love' (Downes/Payne)
This is a strong song and sets the tone for the album in questioning what the

world has become. Payne pulls no punches here:

What about love? And the human race
What about love? It's a different face
What about love?
Why can't we embrace?
I've got to know, I want to know

Even more direct, and with vitriol, Payne says, 'You choose your brother, If he looks the same, You dirty white boy, It's all for gain, But I know what you know, So I won't let this go'. This is quite heavy stuff lyrically, and the downbeat, insistent push of the music accents it with choppy, driving guitars, organ, and steady pounding drums.

Govan has a mind-blowing solo in the outro; his virtuosity is a key element why Asia was able to try different things on this album. The song stops on a dime with a powerful finish.

'What About Love' was issued as a promo single, but radio stations ignored it completely. It was a pity because it was a bold song and sounded of the times. Plus, it sounded strong in concert.

'Long Way From Home' (Downes/Payne)
This selection has a mid-tempo pace with muted, chugging chords. But it's a little too close to Bon Jovi's anthem, 'Living On A Prayer,' in some ways. However, there's a strong and insistent vocal melody on the chorus, making it very accessible. Though chosen as a single, you already know the story: no airplay and no chance of a hit.

There's no good reason for the song to be over six minutes in length, though, and like many songs on the album, some judicious editing would've been most beneficial. This was an issue as the Payne years went along and the band kept extending song running times, to their detriment.

'Midnight' (Downes/Payne)
This song opens with heavy organ and drummer Slade playing low tom fills. After that, it becomes another mid-tempo song with a fairly limp structure overall, the keyboards supplying little more than texture. The chorus is a touch out of place with the overall tone, and it's confusing at this point where exactly the album is headed, though things do improve.

'Midnight' attempts some sort of macabre feel, but it's fairly standard in the end. In the mid-section, there's a jolting change to Uriah Heep and Deep Purple-styled heavy prog rock, with interlocking guitar and keyboard solos and pounding drums and organ. But then it goes right back to that weak chorus as if that section was edited in by accident. There is some quite intriguing stuff going on here, but only in the mid-section. A strange one indeed.

76

'Blue Moon Monday' (Downes/Payne)

Here's one that's a real downer. Lumbering along for over seven minutes, it's a song that drags at times. Downes tosses in more organ parts and occasional synth squeals. The chorus is fairly heavy, in some ways echoing *Arena*'s 'The Day Before The War'. The overall dreary feel is a bit hard to grasp.

There's a lengthy middle part around 4:20, where nothing happens aside from a few traces of acoustic guitar, soothing string synths and Slade's light drum rim touches. Around 5:20, this music continues, but with light organ fills and Slade now playing a backbeat faintly in the mix.

There's not a whole lot going on here, but the song is somewhat entrancing. Some angular hard-hitting chords conclude things, but the track really feels like a mix of something cool with something that doesn't quite jell. It's progressive and detailed, but at the same time, it's a song that overreaches to some degree.

'Silent Nation' (Downes/Payne)

Another long one, the title track opens with tranquil keyboards and audio effects. Then Govan comes in on guitar with octaves and minor chords, while Slade plays a steady drum roll, similar to Carl Palmer. The keyboards are more forceful on this track, Downes once again favouring organ for the most part.

The lyrics are a strong point, with Payne commenting on society and world issues:

It's not up to me
To change what has been done
It's not up to me
A speechless world looks on
It just has to be, Silent nation

After Govan's jazz-like guitar solo, a key change shifts the song to a more dramatic level before things drop back down to a quiet drum shuffle by the always-classy Slade with excellent bass work by Payne. This is one of the album's best moments and is well worth repeated listens. It was also an excellent selection for the tour setlist.

'Ghost In The Mirror' (Downes/Payne/Sherwood)

A pleasant change of pace, this song is instantly infectious right from the snappy opening guitar riff. It's one of two songs here written with Yes member Billy Sherwood, before the regular sessions began for the album; thus it sounds rather different from the other material. (Also on these two tracks is the current Yes drummer, Jay Schellen.)

Despite having a catchy verse and a bridge, the song is quite repetitive, so be prepared for an endless barrage of choruses - a different way of writing, to be sure. But the hooks are well-conceived and the track is still an attractive listen for the most part.

'Gone Too Far' (Downes/Payne)

After the light-hearted 'Ghost in the Mirror', we drop down to the more depressing 'Gone Too Far'. The lyrics are on the side of being overworked and could've been reigned in some. However, despite a number of special things going on in this piece, the listener needs patience, as the beginning is slow to develop.

The intro recalls *Aqua*'s 'The Voice Of Reason', and the keyboards have an almost harp-like quality to them. No matter what the lyrical content, John Payne sings with assuredness, hitting an impressive note at the three-minute mark, before the drums finally surface and Govan's passionate guitar solo brings in more life. But it's not long before the song's original dour nature brings it back down. At nearly seven minutes in length overall, an absolutely phenomenal Govan guitar solo of over two minutes saves the day. This gives way to a chilling monk-like choir, closing the song in eerie fashion.

'Gone Too Far' is certainly one of the most progressive moments on *Silent Nation*, and it's obvious that Payne went all-out in crafting this epic.

'I Will Be There For You' (Downes/Payne/Sherwood)

The other collaboration with Billy Sherwood, 'I Will Be There For You' is a snappy, power-chord-heavy pop/rock song, and it sure rocks. The pre-chorus is filled with hooks, and the chorus itself sounds like a cross between Styx and Foreigner, which is actually a pretty good thing.

Downes hides in the background on this one, only really being heard from in simple pre-chorus parts and faint organ in the chorus. The bridge quietens things down a bit before the track takes on a Survivor-like sound. Govan then unleashes a furious torrent of notes in a blistering minute-long solo that continues right to the last chord.

'Darkness Day' (Downes/Payne)

A moody masterpiece, this gothic slab of progressive rock has modern rock shades and a haunting feel with ominous lyrics. The intro features a choir of monks, conjuring visions of a cathedral before squelching synths bubble up with Slade's pounding drums accompanied by fragmented guitar notes.

Despite an element of modernising techno influence, the track is a bit of a one-trick pony, not really developing beyond the main theme. But it's so large and grand in scale, it doesn't matter. It's all about the atmosphere created, and the track could definitely be used in a futuristic film.

'Darkness Day' is one of those songs that makes you appreciate just how talented John Payne is, and what he was able to bring to all these albums.

'The Prophet' (Downes/Payne)

The John Payne era concludes with this unusual song that starts with whale-like calls, before becoming another darkly-shaded piece. Payne brings wonderful, restrained vocals, and Govan's phenomenal blues soloing simply owns the track.

Downes supplies a nice dose of organ and synths, while Slade's rock-solid drumming echoes his time with The Firm and Uriah Heep. Govan's playing is completely inspired and absolutely addictive.

The lyrics are sparse but thought-provoking, with an obvious religious theme: 'He often wondered where he's from, The Holy Grail, The bloodline son, In his veins the answer comes, The promised land, Parisian'. To hear Payne's development as a singer and lyricist from *Aqua* to *Silent Nation*, is quite something. The final lines are a powerful way to conclude the album:

We sail today
Into the sun
To the place where life began
From the sea
Into the soul
Tell Mother Earth to conquer all

Silent Nation Rarities
'Rise' (Downes/Payne)

This up-tempo and edgy rocker was a bonus track on the Japanese release of *Silent Nation,* and sounds much more like the Asia of *Aria* or *Arena*. Payne sounds great, and Govan's lead harmony part introduces the track along with heavy power chords – his ripping solo around the four-minute mark lasting until the end of fade at 4:46.

The song is unlike anything on *Silent Nation* itself – which is perhaps why it didn't find a place on the album – but it's definitely worth seeking out.

Asia ... *On Track*

The Original Line Up Reforms

After the *Silent Nation* album was largely ignored sales-wise (yet again), it wasn't hard to see that Asia were in trouble.

After completing the 2005 live dates, a new studio album – to be titled *The Architect of Time* – was begun. By this point, Slade had departed (he would later reunite with AC/DC) to be replaced by Jay Schellen. But *The Architect of Time* was never completed.

A meeting in February 2006 would lead to the momentous occasion of the classic, original lineup reforming. John Payne was obviously devastated, and negotiations were necessary as he partly owned the band name after Palmer had signed back his share upon his departure in 1992.

Payne would carry on as Asia Featuring John Payne, and also as a member of GPS, and more recently, Dukes of the Orient. Payne gave his all with Asia and had a lot to be proud of.

In 2010, Payne was asked to sing the Rainbow classic, 'Rainbow Eyes', at the funeral service for Rainbow/Black Sabbath vocalist Ronnie James Dio. Payne said it was very tough on his website, but he was honoured to have been asked.

Bizarrely, Payne featured in animated form on an episode of *Family Guy*, dancing to 'Only Time Will Tell' (the original version with John Wetton, which made no sense at all) in front of an animated Kevin Cronin of REO Speedwagon.

The original Asia lineup of Downes, Howe, Palmer and Wetton, had a successful reunion tour in 2006-2007, restoring pride in the Asia name, leading to the release of their first studio album in 25 long years.

Phoenix (2008)

Personnel:
John Wetton: bass, lead vocals
Steve Howe: electric, acoustic, steel guitars
Geoff Downes: keyboards
Carl Palmer: drums, percussion
Additional musicians: Hugh McDowell (cello on two tracks)
Released: 11 April 2008
Recorded: Liscombe Park (Buckinghamshire, UK) September 2007-February 2008
Producers: Asia, Steve Rispin
Engineer: Steve Rispin
Cover Illustration: Roger Dean
Highest chart position: UK: 166, US: 73, Japan: 27, Germany: 58,
Switzerland: 75

John Wetton, Steve Howe, Geoff Downes and Carl Palmer were back. On 31 August 2006 in Atlantic City, New Jersey, the original lineup played live for the first time in 23 years (though there was a warm-up gig in Rochester, New York, on 29 August). I was at this show and it delivered the goods, exceeding all expectations. The band was thrilled, not only with the fan reaction, but to be enjoying each other once again as people. They only played songs from the first two albums, and for the first time, dipped into their pasts with one song each from Yes, ELP, King Crimson (oddly with a classic song Greg Lake had sung, not Wetton) and The Buggles. There were solos from Howe, Downes and Palmer, as well as an acoustic set. The debut album *Asia* was played in its entirety, although not straight through. UK dates followed in November and December.

In 2007, Asia had a sold-out tour of Japan, also playing Mexico, South America and another summer tour of the US (where this author saw them again in Atlantic City). A live album/DVD of a concert from the Japanese tour was released. But future planned dates for the US, Canada and the UK were scrapped, as Wetton had to undergo open-heart surgery. This threw the new studio album in progress into jeopardy. Unfortunately, Carl Palmer underwent an angioplasty a few months after Wetton's procedure. Thankfully, all turned out well, and somehow the original lineup completed their first studio album since 1983.

'Never Again' (Downes/Wetton)

The clever opening power chords echoing 'Heat of the Moment', announced that Asia were back. Although that song was in C, 'Never Again' is in A minor, giving it a darker sound, and with the lyrical content, that makes sense. The song is a defiant return, and Wetton sounds magnificent vocally. The vintage Asia sound is very much intact right from the start, and the only gripe would be that the drums are mixed too low.

The track show's a feeling of unity amongst the four musicians, and it became one of the few songs from the album to be regularly performed in concert. The chorus seems to have an anti-war theme:

Never again will I bear arms against my brothers
Never again will I dishonour anyone
Never again will I wish evil on another
Never again will I bear arms against my brothers

But apparently, the song was inspired by astrologers who at the time were saying we were entering the age of Gemini, and Wetton was on record as saying that the song summed up a three-year personal odyssey that led up to the new album.

At the time of the album's 2008 release, Wetton said on his website that the chorus was 'a kind of distilled mantra' for the ten commandments. This author would not have picked up on that, but it can certainly be seen as such. 'Never Again' was a stellar opening statement for the album.

'Nothing's Forever' (Wetton)

After an a capella opening featuring layers of John Wetton's voice, a symphonic synth riff opens the song with Palmer's patented snare rolls. The tone is soft and the song is quite tender throughout.

But it's a pretty disappointing choice for the second cut. Palmer's drums are barely even audible – not that he's doing a whole lot – and the song just never develops. But the lyrics are of high quality, with Wetton talking about what we all must face: mortality. The point is to enjoy today because there is no guarantee of tomorrow. Unfortunately, the music takes a back seat and doesn't do the lyrics justice. Howe does a few solos at the end, but even these are fairly standard.

'Heroine' (Downes/Wetton)

There's no doubt that the gift of melody had not escaped the team of Downes and Wetton. Alas, this soft rock song might be better-suited for a Paul Anka album, though it certainly has some sweet melodies. The lyrics may be sincere, but the following stanza is pretty clumsy:

I hold the razor blade to my face
I feel the pulse beneath my skin
The crimson line describes the outer trace
Of my broken heart within

Downes and Wetton have written some gorgeous ballads, and while this is flighty and melodic, the lyrics are too sappy.

Howe plays weepy slide guitar, and Palmer plays as if he's asleep; the whole thing feels as if the band are playing by numbers. Downes wrote the verses, Wetton the chorus, and they combined on the bridge, which is arguably the only decent part. Surprisingly, this was broken out as a live track in 2013 and released on the 2017 live album/DVD, *Symfonia*, where the orchestra gave the song more colour and life.

'Sleeping Giant/No Way Back/Reprise' (Downes/Wetton)

This eight-minute tour de force is the polar opposite of what the original Asia was about in the 1980s. Back then, the band concentrated on doing anything 'but' an epic piece like this. However, this was 25 years later, and if they wanted to let loose and remind us all of their wonderful pasts in bands like Yes, King Crimson and ELP – where an eight-minute song was considered standard – it was okay with the fans.

The opening is magnificent. After Palmer's ominous crashing of a gong, Downes' creepy synth figure comes in, followed by Howe's stinging guitar solos, while a gothic choir of Wetton's voice moans low. Then it's a switch to a sitar/guitar hybrid. This pattern repeats until about 2:43 when the 'No Way Back' segment begins with a strong keyboard sound recalling the first three albums.

In the pre-chorus, a chord sequence occurs that is straight out of *Alpha*'s 'True Colours'. Wetton sings with ease and adds excellent bass fills. There are elements of 'Sole Survivor', 'Open Your Eyes' and 'After The War' in there somewhere: the wonderful ending solo on the 'No Way Back' segment really sounding like Howe's playing on 'Sole Survivor'.

Around the 7:20 mark, Howe plays vintage Yes licks to take the song out. This does not feel at all like eight minutes, and that's a strength. But considering the length, the song probably could've done with a touch more flash. Nonetheless, it's a real highlight.

'Alibis' (Downes/Howe/Palmer/Wetton)

This song – originally known as 'Jodie' – started life in 1983, was worked on during the *Alpha* sessions but not completed. Wetton stated the original title came from manager Brian Lane's wife, who was a big fan of actress Jodie Foster and thought it was time for a song to be written about her. The band didn't like the idea, but Wetton said the name stuck. Although it is now called 'Alibis', the lyrics give a nod to Jodie Foster in lines, 'So Jodie, Maybe this is the last time that I will ever speak your name, I'm going home'. For any die-hard fan, this was a really cool way of acknowledging the past with some cheeky humour.

Musically, the song is pure 1980s, with a richly melodic pop/rock feel exuding all the warmth you'd expect from Asia. It has a sound that is not unlike Journey, Foreigner or Styx, and the keyboards feel like 1983. The chorus is syrupy but undeniably catchy, and Howe lays down classic slide leads and also a killer solo sounding like his inspired playing from the debut album. Palmer's drumming is lively, especially with the chorus' thumping toms and snare. Downes' keyboard solos have that vintage 1980s squeal, and the licks traded with Howe are beautiful.

At 3:50, the song makes a wild change, with Downes playing the harpsichord sounding like it's from an elegant 18th Century banquet. Howe joins in at 4:33 with an extended solo of pure excellence, as Palmer keeps a steady beat. To end the fade, Downes plays a synth solo, sounding like the playing on *Alpha*'s 'My Own Time (I'll Do What I Want)'. 'Alibis' is credited as a group composition and is one of the real *Phoenix* highlights.

'I Will Remember You' (Downes/Wetton)

Here is a fairly sad ballad about loss, with subtle arrangement and a striking chorus. Wetton's brilliant lyric describes the pain of not being over a past love.

Wetton's voice is prominent in the mix, the music largely complementary. This track really shows off Palmer's tasteful play: an element often sadly ignored. There is little guitar besides Howe's eloquent solo. Downes plays with his usual grace, and Hugh McDowell – formerly of ELO – plays the cello as a nice touch. The song deserves to be in a drama or romantic movie.

John Wetton recalled the writing of the song on his website in 2008:

I'm allowing myself a look back over my shoulder with this one, a lament over someone who had a profound effect on me way back when. It's about being so in love you can't think of or do, anything else, and the warm memory of that feeling in retrospect.

In isolation, certain lyrics could be interpreted as being about the loss of someone through death, such as, 'Locked in my memory, Your silhouette, The only face I see, I can't forget', or 'Sometimes I reach for you, But you're not there, The place you take me to, I know not where'. It's pretty obvious that this past love was very strong, but it's also easy to see why someone could relate to it in another way. That's the beauty of great songwriting – it can be left up to the listener to figure out what it truly means to them.

'Shadow Of A Doubt' (Downes/Wetton)

It's certainly fine that Asia would want to place pop songs on an album because they were so good at it back in the day. But this one is a little uninspired. It's a simple, harmless pop tune, with cheesy keyboard fills in an unabashedly 1980s style.

Wetton said on his website that this was a natural successor to 'Don't Cry', both in music and lyrics. But it lacks the charm of that song, and it's not too memorable. It does have a lovely chorus, though and is indeed pleasant, but it doesn't have all that much that's compelling enough to warrant repeated listens.

'Parallel Worlds/Vortex/Deya' (Downes/Wetton)

Not one but 'two' eight-minute epics appear on *Phoenix*, and the album is all the better for it. Much like the album's other suite, this three-part song features a series of instrumental sequences. The 'Parallel Words' section is a moody, effective piece of music that is very open and creates a dreamy atmosphere right away. You can feel a clear night and see the stars as you hear this play out. This segment has great bass parts and backing vocals from Wetton, and Howe's nifty guitar solo really leaps out.

The 'Vortex' segment is very much progressive and in the Yes writing vein. Downes plays crystalline bell-sounding keyboard parts in conjunction with Howe's staccato guitar lines, as Palmer pummels the snare, leading to his cracking drum solo at 4:24. It's not a long solo but is exciting to hear. Then follows the mellow, hypnotic finale.

The final section, 'Deya', is based on an instrumental Wetton began around his Uriah Heep days in 1976 and developed further in 1981 during demos for the *Asia* album. This piece features a melodic lead line, and Howe's guitar work shines, including classical and Spanish styles. Prog fans can rejoice.

'Wish I'd Known All Along' (Howe)

An absolute gem from Steve Howe, this very different style of music for Asia, works like a charm. Tropical, Spanish and classical sounds embellish this one, and there's a cool missed-beat rhythm into the chorus, with Wetton singing in an almost talkative style. He shows a lot of vocal character throughout the song.

The musical backing is perfectly executed, with Downes supplying tropical sounds. His wild synth solo continues to dazzle during the next chorus and is probably his best playing on the album.

Howe shreds some nasty lead guitar tones towards the end, playing with real aggression. In some ways, this song sounds a little like Madonna's 'La Isla Bonita' (and that's actually a good thing). 'Wish I'd Known All Along' is a really strong composition and evidence of the high standard of most of Howe's Asia contributions.

'Orchard Of Mines' (Fayman/Pursey)

Here Asia cover an obscure song, and they do something wonderful with it. 'Orchard of Mines' is by the musical collective that makes up the symphonic rock act, Globus. Their version is an ethereal, moving and spine-tingling masterpiece, particularly when performed live.

Asia pay due respect to the original, and Wetton turns in a tremendous vocal performance, especially at the bridge, where the story protagonist stands up for himself, saying he will not be manipulated in this relationship anymore.

The arrangement here is similar to the Globus one, with a serious accent on dark passages and slight electronic treatments that work excellently within the haunting mood. At times it sounds like something Enigma might have done. If you've never heard Globus, I highly suggest checking out their dark and powerful heavy rock/choir/orchestra/opera mélange.

'Over And Over' (Howe)

This song originated as a Howe demo in the 1980s and was brought to life for *Phoenix*. Steve plays a variety of instruments, including mandolin and pedal steel, adding folk and country into what is an engaging mid-tempo song with excellent structure and melodies. Steve dominates the track, having solos on mandolin, pedal steel and lead guitar. Wetton sings well, Downes has a couple of solos on synth and organ, and Palmer's drumming is steady and lively. Everyone comes together quite nicely on this unheralded track.

Due to the dominant songwriting team of Downes and Wetton, Steve Howe is under-appreciated as an Asia writer. But songs like this and 'Wish I'd Known All Along', go a long way towards the argument that Steve should be more involved in the writing. The fact that he was shut out completely on *Alpha* was unfortunate and short-sighted.

'An Extraordinary Life' (Downes/Wetton)

One of the best lyrics John Wetton has ever written, this inspirational song was also very personal for him. John had not lived the most sober of lives and that affected both his health and his relationships. Eventually, he had to undergo open-heart surgery, which saved his life.

The song was begun prior to all this – while on tour in 2007 – but was completed after the surgery, in time for the album. The theme of the lyric is certainly 'carpe diem', or 'seize the day'. Wetton described the song like this on his website in 2008:

> The concept of carpe diem, or the willingness and ability to 'seize the moment', is key to my decision to appreciate my life today. The chorus was written and demo-recorded at a soundcheck at the State Theater, New Brunswick, NJ, in 2007, and titled on the bus to Asti, Italy, later that summer, just before my spell in surgery. Little did I know it would be such a dramatically accurate omen. A trip to Croatia unlocked the lyric for me.

And what lyrics they are. 'An Extraordinary Life' features many great lines. It's obviously autobiographical but can be inspirational for anyone in any situation. Right from the opening, Wetton is confessional: 'A perfect day, Or so I say, From where I'm standing, This roller coaster ride, Fate will decide the ending'. Wetton had been through rough times in recent years, and he knew some of it was self-inflicted. So to come forward in the lyrics and acknowledge such a thing was brave.

The chorus fills the heart and declares, 'Go seize the day, Wake up and say, This is an extraordinary life, Enjoy today, Come what may, This is an extraordinary life'.

In the bridge, we see Wetton coming to terms with how things have gone in life and how they can and will change:

86

All of the good times and all of the bad
Responsibility is totally mine I know
I rightly stand accused
But I believe that I can change
Yes I can change my world

The soaring yet subtle arrangement supports the message with beauty. It's no wonder this song is considered an Asia classic: all the hallmarks are there. Why it wasn't a single – and was tucked away as the album's last song – remains a head-scratcher. However, for a while, it was utilised in a positive way on the popular TV show *America's Got Talent*.

Palmer, Downes and Wetton offer sympathetic playing, and Steve's guitar solo adds to the inspirational feel. Hugh McDowell's cello is low in the mix but blends in with the guitars and keyboards effectively. Even though the song is five minutes long, you wish it would go on longer. This song was a concert staple and one of the few tracks from *Phoenix* to be played live.

'An Extraordinary Life' is heartbreaking in light of the fact that John would pass away just a decade later. However, to know he did change his life and left behind a song and message such as this, is as good as it gets. His voice, talent and spirit, will never be forgotten.

Phoenix Rarities
'I Will Remember You' (acoustic remix) (Downes/Wetton)
This version was a bonus track on the European edition of *Phoenix*. The song takes on a more sombre tone, with an accent on piano and cello, and Wetton's voice is exposed in its frailty and genuine emotion. It's interesting to hear and could certainly be played at a funeral.

'An Extraordinary Life' (acoustic remix) (Downes/Wetton)
While any version of this song is welcome, this acoustic arrangement does the song little justice. Much of the glory and majesty is lost in this style, and the song lacks what made it special in the first place. This is most likely what the guys would've done with it in an MTV Unplugged setting.

Omega (2010)

Personnel:
John Wetton: bass, vocals
Steve Howe: electric, acoustic and steel guitars
Geoff Downes: keyboards
Carl Palmer: drums, percussion
Released: 21 April 2010
Recorded: Liscombe Park (Buckinghamshire, UK) October 2009-February 2010
Producer: Mike Paxman
Engineer: Steve Rispin
Cover Illustration: Roger Dean
Highest Chart Position: UK: 135, Japan: 29, Germany: 56, Switzerland: 55

The 2008 and 2009 tours – where they played in North America, Europe and Japan – featured shows that were even better than the reunion tour. More songs from *Alpha* were in the set, and one from *Astra* snuck in there too. But they were no longer playing every cut from the debut album. The band kept the four songs from their previous bands in the set, which took away from playing extra new material. Surprisingly, only two songs from *Phoenix* were performed.

Opening the shows with 'Daylight' was a complete shocker, but a great choice. In 2009, the band returned to North America, co-headlining with Yes. Steve Howe played with both bands, an exhausting setup that he bravely maintained for each show. The band also filmed a 2009 UK show that would be released in 2011. Later in 2009, the news was announced that another studio album was on the way for 2010.

By this point, the original Asia lineup was now on its fourth year back together, which was longer than they lasted after first forming in 1981. *Omega* was, in many ways, a much stronger album with more overall vigour than *Phoenix*, which had some filler and a softer mix and feel. Perhaps it was the fact that both Wetton and Palmer were back to full health that led to such inspired playing and writing. From start to finish, this was one of the best Asia albums by any lineup.

The album was also Asia's second on the respected Frontiers label. But where *Phoenix* was distributed by EMI, *Omega* did not have the same fortune, and the album was unavailable in the US for a few months, forcing fans to seek out import copies at first, which is why it failed to chart in America. Thankfully this would not happen again with the label.

The tour concerts were excellent. The band proudly played five songs from the new album and maintained two from *Phoenix* along with classics from the first three albums. They no longer needed to do songs from their previous bands.

'Finger On The Trigger' (Downes/Wetton)
The album opener is a rocker with meaty power chords and crisp drumming: this time pronounced in the mix. Carl Palmer hadn't been heard this

prominently on an Asia album in a long time. Downes' organ swirls around the guitars, and Wetton sounds great, his voice having gotten a little huskier in the reunion era.

'Finger On The Trigger' originally surfaced on the second iCon album – *iCon II: Rubicon* – that Wetton and Downes did back in 2006. The arrangement isn't too dissimilar here, and the melody is the same. But the Asia version is more aggressive. It's fun hearing Howe rock out once in a while. The song has hooks galore, and the verse is every bit as memorable as the pre-chorus and chorus. Additionally, Wetton's backing vocals sound rich and detailed in those sections.

Wetton said in press interviews to promote the new album, rather humorously, that the song was 'an overtly sexual reference'. Howe's outro solo is perfectly placed, in line with the musical theme, and even though it seems like it's headed for a fade, the song comes to an end. Live, this one went over very well, every night of the tour.

'Through My Veins' (Howe/Wetton)

Sometimes a song just reaches a listener instantly, taking effect in a deep way from the opening chord. 'Through My Veins' is a haunting work, with a nice mixture of major and minor chords, some faint but effective keyboard sequencing, and deep lyrical content.

When Steve Howe gets involved in the writing of Asia songs, not only are these some of the band's best compositions, but they also allow for stellar performances from John Wetton. Whatever problems the two had in the past, it certainly didn't destroy their musical chemistry. Not all the best Asia songs are Wetton/Downes compositions.

There are some beautiful chord choices here. Wetton has some deep lyrics and the opening verse is rich with imagery:

Invisible sun cast your shadow over me
As wind cuts like a knife
Catapulting me from life with you
Waiting on an empty street
Hiding from the sun

The music marries to the words, and the mood prevails throughout. Wetton effectively uses vocal inflexion to accent certain words, which indeed marries with Howe's guitar fills, Downes' keyboard touches, and Palmer's steady rhythm.

But Howe and Wetton are the stars of the show. Wetton's harmony vocals at the end of the chorus are brilliant, and Downes plays lovely cinematic-sounding keyboard flurries over the outro sequence. His subtle keyboard blips accompanying Steve's guitar shapes in the mid-section only add to the delicacy. There are no lyrics for the last 90 seconds or so, and Palmer's cymbal crashes over the last few hanging chords are dynamic.

'Through My Veins' was played live on the *Omega* tour, and it was as good as expected, with fans knowing the song well. The live version on *Resonance* is outstanding. In this writer's opinion, 'Through My Veins' is an all-time Top 10 Asia song.

'Holy War' (Downes/Wetton)
Asia give progressive rock fans a six-minute blast with the religion-themed 'Holy War'. Featuring thunderous musical moments and a memorable chorus, this song ranks up there with past Asia epics such as 'Wildest Dreams', 'Open Your Eyes', 'After The War' and 'Parallel Worlds/Vortex/Deya'.

The song opens with cinematic piano and crashing chords before the verses begin. Palmer's drumming is exceptional here and throughout the album: he hadn't sounded this invigorated in the studio in years. The soaring chorus is vintage Asia, and the lyrics are timely.

Howe has a scathing guitar solo around the three-minute mark, before Palmer's drum arsenal delivers triumphantly for a good 30 seconds or so: keyboards and guitars swirling all around (this is where you can hear a nod to 'Wildest Dreams'). The ending is ominous and dark, letting us know that despite the many problems, there is still no resolution to these conflicts.

The chorus repeats, 'Oh, oh holy war, It's what we're fighting for, And is it worth dying for?'. While numerous artists have tackled this subject over the years, the approach here is direct, but not heavy-handed. One especially good verse hits hard emotionally: 'And when the battle line, Becomes a holy shrine, We shout, 'God wills it!', At the city wall'.

'Holy War' was an explosive number when played live: the audience anticipating Palmer's drum sequence, applauding with fervour during the song. This song stayed in the set for several years and is an outstanding moment in the original band's second incarnation.

'Ever Yours (Semper Fidelis)' (Downes/Wetton)
While it was standard practice for Asia albums to include ballads, they became increasingly fewer in the reunion era. But 'Ever Yours' is so saccharine and easy-listening that it is tough to sit through. Asia ballads can be strong and moving, or they can go the other way, becoming as fluffy as a pillow. The latter is the case here.

Lyrically, things are pretty weak, with lines such as this standing out: 'What are the chances we would ever meet, If I were vagabond and you were royal?'. The music is bland, with Downes, Palmer and Howe not taking part at all with any feeling. But who could blame them? There was nothing much to do. Surprisingly, the song appeared in the live set a few times in 2013.

Semper Fidelis, by the way, translates as 'Always Faithful': the official motto of the US Marine Corps.

'Listen, Children' (Downes/Wetton)
Here is an expertly crafted pop/rock song with a great sense of euphoria and

celebration of life. There is plenty to like: it's definitely a hook-laced track but also includes progressive rock hints. Wetton's voice, and the jaunty hook, compliment the upbeat feel.

The song came largely from Downes, though Wetton wrote the melody and lyrics. The lyric was based on Wetton observing a group of children playing on a grassy hill without a care in the world in France on a summer night in 1992. He stated on his website that the song's mood was inspired by the Grateful Dead classic, 'Uncle John's Band', and the chorus by the Kansas song, 'Carry on Wayward Son', adding that the song sounds absolutely nothing like either of those.

Downes' keyboard intro sets up the inspirational nature of the song, and as soon as the bass and drums kick in, it becomes even more uplifting. That chorus is classic Wetton, and his harmony vocals are a joy. Howe isn't heard from until the three-minute mark, where he solos extensively – before and after a shiny keyboard sweep with stabbing chords.

It's a shame this song never made it to the live arena. Even on your worst day, it's pretty tough not to feel good hearing this gem.

'End Of The World' (Downes/Wetton)
Not as much of a downer as one might expect from the title, 'End Of The World' is another excellent track with an outstanding Wetton vocal performance. It starts with a bombastic keyboard flourish and some leads from Howe before mellowing out into a mid-tempo pace.

John stated on his website that this was his favourite song on the album, so it's no surprise it was played on the 2010 tour. The lyrics are about Wetton overcoming his demons.

> And the grinding wheels are turning ever
> I believe that God is love, and that's enough
> To keep the evil demon away
> Don't say I don't matter at all
> I will stand or I will fall
> You're the most important call that I make
> When I face that verdict today
> Though it's Auto-da-Fe
> I'll say it's really not the end of the world

'Auto-da-Fe' more or less means an act of faith, and that's what Wetton is referencing here. As for the music, Howe plays a sweet solo towards the end, over what are well-chosen chord changes. Another great song on what is becoming a really strong album.

'Light The Way' (Howe/Wetton)
A bold, fat synth figure opens proceedings, grabbing the listener's attention immediately. Howe mixes in some snarling slide leads, and when Wetton and

Palmer join in, it becomes a breakneck-paced high energy pop-rocker with a superior melody.

The chorus changes tempo with Wetton's voice layers singing, 'No matter what it is, Be sure it can be fixed, Letting go of yesterday might, just might, light the way'. The spirit of many Asia songs is uplifting, and 'Light The Way' also carries that feeling. The mid-section has a brief organ breakdown from Downes before the tempo leaps up again, Howe then adding more leads. A series of odd chords then leads to a key change and a ripping solo from Howe, while Palmer's drumming becomes creative and active.

A few orchestral chord blasts lead to a series of choruses, with Wetton reaching high before Howe cracks out another ear-piercing slide solo in the outro. Palmer switches from hi-hat to ride cymbal and toms, giving the arrangement shape. Those types of dynamics are a key part of Asia's writing. 'Light the Way' was built for the live stage, but for whatever reason, it never made the cut.

'I'm Still The Same' (Downes/Wetton)
There's a significant Beatles, Beach Boys and ELO influence on this one, not to mention a dash of XTC. It's quite a snappy, sunny pop tune, with some good moments. But it does tend to get repetitive and seems to be missing a little something.

That being said, it's extremely perky, and the key change at the end is quite fetching. Maybe it would have benefited from separating the verses and choruses a bit to break up the monotony. Wetton sounds great, though, and Howe is at home with the jazz fills he throws in.

'There Was A Time' (Downes/Wetton)
This splendid mini-epic is downright chilling. Wetton sings of a tortured heart that is trying to figure out what went wrong with an ex. Downes' ghostly piano and Howe's regal classical guitar, supply the moody, evocative feel.

Once the drums kick in, Palmer plays a shuffle beneath Howe's atmospheric guitar licks, which would not sound out of place on a Pink Floyd record. Though Downes' piano solo is wonderful, the track never gets bright and sunny, and nor should it.

The protagonist does not seem to be over her, but he certainly has some thoughts he'd like to share with her:

There was a time when I loved you
And a time when I lied
There were none up above you
And for you, I'd have died
But the big wheel turns at last
When all my emotions were tied up with you
My hopes and my dreams could never win through

The path has been cleared, now I'm free of you
Yeah, now is my time

Heavy sentiments indeed, and something we can all relate to. After that final
chorus (the lyrics change in each chorus, which is rather clever), there's still
one final line: 'There will come a time for you'. You know he's really saying,
'She's going to get what's coming, eventually!'.

'I Believe' (Downes/Wetton)
One of the last songs composed for the album, 'I Believe' is vintage Asia. It's
another spirited anthem in the vein of 'An Extraordinary Life': intended to
uplift and accent the positives of life and living.
    Wetton gets introspective once more, digging down deep to declare that he
won't be caving in and will be fighting on. Right in the opening verse, Wetton
declares:

Staring at the blue horizon, do I have a choice?
Seeing life in the negative, for sure I will fall
Somewhere deep inside of me
I hear a tiny voice
Saying that's it's not a dead-end street after all

The music sounds like it could've appeared on either of the first two albums,
and the band are in total unison: something you can just feel with each
passage. The group selected this one to be played live, and it blended in
perfectly. In fact, it was the opening number on the 2010 tour, always followed
by 'Only Time Will Tell'. It felt like they were from the same album, not 28
years apart.
    The chorus states: 'I believe that we have one chance at success, I believe
that love is the key to happiness, Yes, I believe'. The Downes/Wetton team
had come through yet again, with another great song and another simple but
important and heartfelt message.

'Don't Wanna Lose You Now' (Downes/Wetton)
A pleasant enough, laid-back pop number, this song is a bit on the safer side
of things. It feels more like filler than anything that really needed to be on
the album. The verses are fairly average, and though the chorus works well
enough, it's all rather slight.
    Howe has a brief solo break which simply just relays the melody for a few
notes. Palmer and Downes both haven't got much to do. There are nods to The
Beatles and Beach Boys again at times, especially at the end when a distinctive
Beatles feel comes in with the chords and trumpet-like keyboards. As an album
closer, it's mildly disappointing but doesn't take away from *Omega*'s overall
strength.

The *Omega* tour of 2010/2011 spawned another live DVD/CD, this one recorded in Basel, Switzerland in 2010. It was far better than the *Phoenix* tour's live in Cambridge CD/DVD.

After the tour, the band broke for solo activities, and in the case of Howe and Downes, a return to Yes. But another Asia studio album was on the way for 2012, and it was to be not only the best of the reunion era but one of the best Asia albums ever.

Omega Rarities
'Emily' (Downes/Wetton)
'Emily' only appeared on the US version of *Omega*, and it made the record worse for it. The song was tucked into the middle of the album: odd for a bonus track, although Wetton was fond of the song and did not consider it to be a bonus cut.

It's a cheeky pop song about a woman Wetton was taken with, who he found out was gay. But he took the situation in good humour and made it into a song. But the lyrics are rather painful and ridiculous:

As you glide to the sea, you are pure divinity
In my head was your bed and your femininity
But the pain is insane now that everyone can see
It just ain't meant to be, Emily

'Drop A Stone' (Downes/Howe/Palmer/Wetton)
Appearing only on the Japanese release, this bonus track is more of a blues-based song and thus out of character for Asia. Wetton initially wanted a Pink Floyd feel for the song, but that is clearly not what happened.

The song has a dirty, gritty feel, with Wetton's vocal and Howe's guitar taking prominence. It's not common to hear Steve attacking his guitar like this with either Asia or Yes, but he certainly can play the blues. He throws in some country licks along the way, and you can hear the influence of Chet Atkins, Eric Clapton, Peter Green and Les Paul.

But does it work as an Asia track? No, and that's why it's a bonus cut and a quirky one. The joint writing credits indicate this probably originated from a band jam, and that's quite the feel the song gives off. It's fun hearing the band let loose like this in what was clearly a break from the norm.

XXX (2012)

Personnel:
John Wetton: bass, vocals
Steve Howe: electric, acoustic and steel guitars
Geoff Downes: keyboards
Carl Palmer: drums, percussion
Released: 20 June 2012
Recorded: Liscombe Park (Buckinghamshire, UK) January-March 2012
Producer: Mike Paxman
Engineer: Steve Rispin
Cover Illustration: Roger Dean
Highest Chart Position: US: 134, UK: 69, Japan: 36, Germany: 33, Switzerland: 43

XXX was to be the final studio album for the original lineup, so they made it count and then some. From beginning to end, this album is simply outstanding. There is much detail in the songs, not to mention the best production, engineering and mixing job yet for the reunion albums. There is a richness and detail to the performances and writing that clearly shows they really wanted to make the best album possible.

Roger Dean stepped it up with a beautiful cover illustration featuring the dragon and orb from the debut album 30 years prior. On the Chinese calendar, 2012 was the Year of the Water Dragon, and with 2012 also being the thirtieth anniversary of the debut album, it all tied in, making the Roman numeral for thirty, appropriate as the title – *XXX*. The cover's colour scheme, utilising sea green, orange, red, dark green and pink, was eye-catching. The colour scheme also connected to the feel of the music, which was simply excellent.

The chemistry was there. Everyone was in unison and feeling very good about the album as it was about to be released and another tour was to start. Asia had made an album to be proud of. Though it turned out to be the final one for the original lineup, they had achieved everything they'd set out to, and then some, with the reunion going way longer than anyone could've imagined.

'Tomorrow The World' (Downes/Wetton)
What a strong opener this one is. After a poignant piano intro, the song becomes a driving rocker in full-on Asia style, with pumping piano, muted guitar chords, forceful drums, and those wonderful Wetton vocals.

The song begins with the chorus, and then the main theme comes in from Downes on keyboards. It's not until the second set of verses that Howe starts adding guitar leads in between the lyric lines. Wetton adds harmonies on certain parts of the bridge and verses, accenting the last word of a sequence.

Howe has a fiery solo, while Downes adds a few synths before it's back to another bridge. The song concludes with a repeat of the opening chorus, allowing Downes and Howe to fill in with leads while Palmer throws down double-time drumming, giving way to a final scalding lead from Howe.

The song suddenly ends with an organ solo and a final hanging chord. This is as good as anything on the debut album, and to be honest, *XXX* never lets up in excellence from here. 'Tomorrow The World' was a fantastic concert number and an example of how fruitful the reunion era was.

'Bury Me In Willow' (Downes/Wetton)

You can't help but feel a twinge of sadness hearing 'Bury Me In Willow' now, after John Wetton's passing in early 2017. The song was written and recorded in 2012, by which point Wetton had overcome many obstacles, including serious health issues.

This song wasn't intended to be a downer; in fact, it was quite the opposite. Wetton had stated that he'd written the chorus and worked it up on a twelve-string guitar (though that instrument was not ultimately played on the recording). He had the idea to be buried in a willow casket, and not the typical oak, when his time came.

On his website when discussing the writing of the tracks on *XXX* Wetton said:

I'll make sure that in death, I forego all the status symbols, pomp and rigmarole of a formal funeral for a pauper's burial. So, the lyric then wrote itself around the chorus. Geoff's music on the verse, solos and outro, my little madcap bridge, and it is superbly orchestrated by Geoff with a brilliant E-bow solo from Steve.

This really is a unique song, and Wetton sings gloriously. The music is contemporary-sounding, and the blend of piano, dainty keyboards, steadily galloping drums and muted guitar is the appropriate choice for the verses. Downes adds some organ before the chorus kicks in, and there are plenty of vocal harmonies. Though the track runs to six minutes, it's not remotely dull and uses its time wisely. It's disappointing this one wasn't played live, but with so many albums to choose from, some songs just don't find their way into the setlist.

'No Religion' (Downes/Howe/Wetton)

This tight and brisk rocker takes no prisoners, lyrically or musically. Heavy power chords introduce the song and continue through the verses. Despite the title, this song is not anti-religious but relates to many people who have been disenfranchised in recent years, losing their jobs, livelihoods and more.

The lyric sees the protagonist very down about life:

Got no religion, just living hell
If I had money, I'd drop it all in the wishing well
Stand in the doorway, wait for a man to come,
Got no religion, and my life's just begun

Wetton said in interviews at the time the album came out that the character is waiting for 'The man', who he believes will give him the goods he needs. But instead, 'The man' tells him how to change his life and get on with it.

Howe's guitars have real grit, but it's Downes who gets a solo, on synth in the middle section. After that, things get creative, as Wetton repeats the sole line 'Got no religion'. Downes accompanies on piano, with some ghostly choir-like voices, as Palmer adds cymbal washes. Howe gives a snaky solo as the rest of the band come back in, leading to the next verse.

The outro features some aggressive Howe soloing, with Downes interlocking on synth and organ for a rollicking finale. In another example of first-class arranging, the song ends with just piano and the one chorus line again repeated. Potentially a great live song: sadly, it was not performed.

'Faithful' (Downes/Wetton)

One of the obligatory ballads, this song is arranged differently, and it works rather well. The opening verses sound almost synth-pop, but the choruses rush in, cascading melodies over the listener, and Wetton sings from the heart. Palmer and Howe add the key ingredients, causing the song to stand out more than some of the band's recent ballads.

Despite being nearly six minutes long, the track doesn't over-extend itself. The chorus pulls at the heartstrings and is instantly memorable. Howe's guitar solo, which repeats the vocal melody, is tear-inducing, his later solo moving away from the melody, as Palmer kicks in with some drum fills. This is no typical ballad and becomes a beautiful, upbeat rocker in the second half.

Combined, Wetton and Downes craft truly insistent melodies. 'Faithful' is a wonderful song. The sentiment is simple, but eloquent:

I'll be faithful, That's what I do
Ever faithful, My aim is true
Wherever you may go, You'll always know
Faithful I'll be with you

The music video for 'Faithful' showed the band in the studio, with moody lighting and a mix of colour and black and white footage.

'I Know How You Feel' (Downes/Wetton)

The next track up is moody, with its spiky keyboard eighth-note stabs and lyrics showing the protagonist offering comfort to someone else in the same position. There's a chilly feel and it's an interesting composition with regards to the structure.

Wetton carries the song with an emotional vocal performance, and the chord changes are seductive. It's no wonder they played this live, although it was always stripped down to just keyboard and vocal in concert. Wetton supplies quality bass licks along the way, while Howe and Palmer offer mostly supplemental playing, performed with taste and precision.

The bonus alternate mix is captivating and highly recommended, showing how in command of his voice Wetton still was at this late-career stage.

'Face On The Bridge' (Downes/Wetton)

Another outstanding track, 'Face On The Bridge,' was inspired by Prague's Charles Bridge, which is lit up at night and is famous for its statues and sketch artists. The song cruises along at a brisk pace, and the chorus chord and vocal arrangements are on the money. If you listen carefully, you can hear Wetton's cell phone ringing over the intro. On the second set of verses, Downes throws in effective, swirling synth licks, and Palmer really kicks things into motion during the choruses and bridge. Howe has a few zippy solos, especially from 5:22 to 5:52. Mike Paxman turns in his best Asia production job yet on this album, and Mark 'Tufty' Evans' mix is outstanding.

'Face On The Bridge' is another reunion-era song that would not have sounded out of place on the debut album. It was *XXX*'s lead single, was supported by a music video, and became a tour fan favourite.

'Al Gatto Nero' (Downes/Wetton)

Loosely translated, the Italian phrase 'al gatto nero' means, 'to the black cat'. But that has nothing to do with this song, as it's actually named after an Italian restaurant Wetton liked that was near his home. Downes wrote the music, and Wetton the lyrics, including the Italian lines which he had a friend translate for him.

Howe plays with a liquid tremolo guitar effect, and Palmer gets in some safe intro drum licks before bursting out with creativity and panache in the intro repeat after the guitar solo.

If there's a weak track on *XXX*, this song qualifies. The chorus has good qualities, but the verses feel a bit lackadaisical, and when Wetton sings the Italian lines, it comes off a bit on the awkward side.

'Judas' (Downes/Howe/Wetton)

It's not often you get a jaunty song with such lyrics in the chorus as 'Why did you choose to stand behind me, Somewhere I couldn't see, Just when I couldn't feel it coming, You put a knife in me'. But it's an insistent, catchy pop/rock song (more rock than pop) with the hooks you'd expect, carrying scathing and vitriolic lyrics. One verse, in particular, is quite sinister: 'I'd love to know what does it feel like, To be a Judas friend, To be a brutal traitor of the soul, Murderous at the end'. Wetton did not say who it was written about, but it sure seems personal. So I'm guessing whoever this Judas is might know it's about them!

Howe brought the backbone of the song to the band, and Downes and Wetton developed it from there. The music is strong, with many power chords, vocal harmonies and excellent solos, including some 1980s-style synth licks from Downes.

'Ghost Of A Chance' (Downes/Wetton)

An emotional powerhouse, this song is an appropriate closer to the album. It starts as a classic Asia ballad with piano and vocals (the melody and arrangement reminding me of 'The Last To Know' from *Alpha*) before Howe adds a quiet, reflective and jazz-like solo that leads to the next piano and vocal verse.

At around 2:08, the drums and a crying slide guitar solo take charge, symphonic keyboards embellishing shortly thereafter. Around 3:00, Howe kicks his slide solo up to another level as the song builds and builds with keyboards and a haunting choir. Wetton comes back in around 3:50 to finish things off.

This song deserved a powerful ending, but it just kind of halts, which is the only complaint here. Otherwise, it's an excellent piece of music that should've been played live.

XXX Rarities

'Reno (Silver And Gold)' (Howe/Wetton)

A bonus track on the deluxe edition of the album, 'Reno (Silver and Gold)' opens with a brief pseudo-Spanish intro and sits as a fairly mellow track throughout. But the song never really sparks significantly, although there is a nice a cappella vocal towards the end. It makes sense this was a bonus track.

'I Know How You Feel (Midnight Mix)' (Downes/Wetton)

This is one of those rare moments when an alternate mix used as a bonus track actually works very well. This 'Midnight Mix' has layers of mood and gives the song a haunting feel. Downes' keyboards weave a spell over the listener as Wetton sings with restraint and beautifully so. Some faint background crashing noises add to the chill, and Howe plays a striking acoustic guitar solo, making this superior to the album version. This was also on the deluxe edition of *XXX*.

'Faithful (Orchestra Version)' (Downes/Wetton)

And then there are alternate versions that don't add much to the picture, such as this one. The album version is far superior to this take. Without Howe and Palmer's parts, the song loses a lot, and the orchestral parts aren't anything imaginative. This version appeared as a bonus cut in Japan only.

Howe Departs

Asia hit the road in 2012 for their 35th-anniversary tour, delivering the goods once again (the *Live in San Francisco* CD/DVD would be issued in 2015). But a short time after the tour ended in January 2013, Howe announced his retirement from the band, as the heavy workload of Asia, Yes and his solo activities had become too much. But the original lineup reunion had lasted from 2006 to 2012, and all the tours, four studio albums and four live albums/ DVDs, were a gift any Asia fan may not have thought was possible.

However, Asia was not done yet, as they reached out to guitarist Paul Gilbert from hard rock group Mr. Big (successful in the 1990s but still together). But Gilbert couldn't accept the offer. However, he did recommend a young guitar player named Sam Coulson. He had little experience, but Asia had found their new guy. Gilbert had discovered him via YouTube and Coulson was quite a find. He toured Europe with the band in 2013, making his debut that summer. One more studio album would be on the way from the band.

Gravitas (2014)

Personnel:
John Wetton: bass, acoustic guitars, vocals
Sam Coulson: guitars
Geoff Downes: keyboards
Carl Palmer: drums
Additional musicians: Katinka Kleijn (cello on one track)
Released: 19 March 2014
Recorded: Liscombe Park (Buckinghamshire, UK) October-December 2013
Producers: John Wetton, Geoff Downes
Engineers: Steve Rispin, Rob Aubrey (vocal engineering)
Cover Illustration: Roger Dean
Highest Chart Position: US: 159, UK: 92, Japan: 42, Germany: 51, Switzerland: 24

In spring 2014, Asia issued their last studio album to date, *Gravitas*. Initially, it was to be titled *Valkyrie*. The record marked the debut of guitarist Sam Coulson. This time, Downes and Wetton produced, making this the first Asia album from the predominantly classic personnel, with no outside producer.

The end result was a mixed bag, with only about half the album measuring up. The mix is fairly limp and Palmer's drums are neutered. There are some songs where Coulson has little to do other than interject a solo, but when he gets his chance, he truly shines, proving to be an excellent acquisition for the band.

All the songs are Downes/Wetton compositions, including one they dug up from 1986 to revisit. Overall, the album was a disappointment but still had a few excellent tracks.

Another tour followed, the band sounding quite good with Coulson, although only two *Gravitas* tracks made their way into the setlist. Sadly, this was to be the last Asia studio album to date, although, in 2016, they were working on material that was never completed after Wetton passed away.

'Valkyrie' (Downes/Wetton)

Opening with a cappella voice layers, this song is rather gloomy and languishes in a fog for nearly six minutes. There are really cool segments, however, and the song will stick with you through the journey. Palmer plays heavy drums, though they are repressed in the mix, and Coulson has a screeching solo that doesn't last long enough.

There is a gothic feel of mystical battles and Scandinavian lands. Wetton's vocals give an eerie feel and the song is somewhat foreboding. It gallops a little too long at the same pace and seems to aspire to higher heights than it achieves. The moaning cello-playing of Katinka Kleijn adds a sombre tone. Maybe this was Asia's grandiose Viking cry, but it feels like it needed something more to really make it stand out.

'Valkyrie' was to be one of two songs here played live on the subsequent tour and proved to be more vivid and powerful in the live setting.

'Gravitas' (Downes/Wetton)
(I.) Lento (II.) Gravitas

The title cut is an eight-minute epic. A lengthy keyboard bed, bordering on new age music, opens the piece but goes on a bit too long. The song lifts eventually but has a dark edge. The choruses are too big and too many, and the lyrics are weak, though Palmer's drumming is strong at times.

Downes uses a lot of organ, giving the song some old-school progressive rock spice. When Coulson is finally heard – from around the seven-minute mark – he shreds like a demon. It's an extremely fiery solo, but otherwise, he is once again relegated to a few muted chords that chug along, much like on 'Valkyrie'.

Although the song doesn't always work, it's a pretty bold effort and worthy of repeated listens. In fact, it would have been a better album opener than 'Valkyrie' and seeing as it is the title cut, it's odd that it wasn't. The band played this song live on the subsequent tour.

'The Closer I Get to You' (Downes/Wetton)

A depressing ballad with some puerile lyrics, 'The Closer I Get to You' is a lowlight, failing to connect with the listener. The chorus is far too layered and huge, especially considering the droll verses that precede it. At six minutes in length, it is an exercise in futility. Lyrically, it's a nadir for Wetton, who offers lines such as, 'There is no answer, no question, no lie, I'm losing count of days passing by, It's like cancer, it's consuming my soul, Nothing there, nothing left, should I die'. Comparing a struggling relationship with cancer is a tasteless analogy. This is one of the weakest songs that Wetton and Downes ever wrote together and is a tough one to grasp.

'Nychtophobia' (Downes/Wetton)

Lightening the mood, this song shows some humour as it explores a man with fear of the night. Amusing lyrics are sprinkled throughout and the song is quite unusual for Asia.

It's fairly standard commercial rock, and Coulson again has a fluid, scorching solo that seems to come out of nowhere, with little input otherwise. Coulson is a quality player whose solos are played with consideration and thought. It's easy to hear why the band selected him.

Unfortunately, Palmer's drums continue to be buried in the mix, and the song is very repetitive with one chorus after another for several minutes until the conclusion. At least the track tries something different, and it is decent enough, despite its flaws.

'Russian Dolls' (Downes/Wetton)

Here is a bizarre song I can't get a handle on. While the melodies are romantic and there are lush sounds on display, it sounds like it was recorded inside a cardboard box. Palmer sounds like he's clapping two pillows together, and

Coulson – barely in the mix at all – is more like an innocent bystander. He might play four or five notes for the whole song.

The arrangement is oddly delicate and it sounds very little like Asia music should sound. The lyrics are fairly cloying, especially the chorus: 'And when you're there, well then, I'm not so cold, When we're alone again, As close as Russian dolls'. It's not clear what any of it means, but the song is so unusual – and the mix so weird – that it has a kind of artsy appeal for me. Little happens from start to finish, and yet the feel and scant production compel me. It's an interesting stylistic choice but is probably better suited for an iCon album.

'Heaven Help Me Now' (Downes/Wetton)
(I.) Wings Of Angels, (II.) Prelude, (III.) Heaven Help Me Now

Arranged in a suite structure, 'Heaven Help Me Now' is really just a long pop/rock song with big, booming choruses and is not very progressive at all, aside from Downes' eloquent classical intro. One might expect a Yes-styled epic from the three parts, but one would be wrong.

The keyboard intro is the only progressive part, and we finally get to hear Palmer's drumming clearer in the mix. Once more, Coulson is relegated to muted power chords and what is becoming standard for him: a flashy solo that drops in and then drops out. Some of the solos – especially that one – sound patched in, almost as if some of the songs were basically done when he joined.

In any case, this song ends up a mild success but fails to attain enough quality parts. The lyrics on this album overall are a major letdown from a writer of Wetton's calibre.

'I Would Die for You' (Downes/Wetton)

Written in 1986, this one came from unused Downes and Wetton material, and it sounds like it. The lyrics are very weak and there aren't many of them. There are only two verses, and the rest are all choruses that simply repeat the title. It seems like it may have taken only ten minutes to write, at least lyrically. Coulson has to settle for those muted chords once again, but at least Palmer is given a smidgen more to do.

After the big 1980s chorus, there is a brief break with a few crunchy notes from Coulson in tandem with Palmer laying down tricky double-kick fills. But that's about all there is of interest. The vocals are strong in the chorus, but to be honest, this sounds like some of the lacklustre early 1990s Payne-era tracks.

In the end, the song returns to the short riff and suddenly fades – gone in barely three minutes. A B-side at best, 'I Would Die For You' has some nice vocal work, but not much else going for it. The demo version does not differ too much from what ended up on the album and can be found on the 2002 demo compilation titled *Wetton-Downes*.

'Joe DiMaggio's Glove' (Downes/Wetton)

A pretty sentiment, but a sappy one, and the title alone is pure schmaltz. The opening vocal melody and guitar parts are right out of the killer Rainbow ballad, 'Tearin' Out My Heart'. Most likely, it was an innocent nick, but it's there for sure.

The style is adult contemporary, and the mix is meek, with the drums and guitars saying little. Coulson has a brief solo, and Downes adds organ parts, but the accent is on the vocals and the corny lyrics: 'I've never been completely lost, I've never been so in love, How did my heart become so soft, Like Joe DiMaggio's glove'. Asia have many good ballads, but – to use baseball terms – this one is a huge swing and a miss, or perhaps a foul ball.

Apparently, John Wetton thought enough of legendary baseball player, Joe DiMaggio, to name a song after him. Although, as it turns out, the band doesn't really watch or understand baseball! I wanted to like this one, I really did, but it's soft rock at best.

'Till Will We Meet Again' (Downes/Wetton)

Ending the album on a serious high note, the band comes up trumps with 'Till We Meet Again'. The song is a mix of folk, pop, rock and even a little Celtic music. Strummed acoustic guitars and Palmer hitting two pounding drum beats bring to mind a bunch of vagabonds marching through the streets, singing their anthem. Eventually, the rest of the band chimes in, with a few low synth notes from Downes and Palmer picking up the drum pace. The layered chorus repeating the title is inspirational and shows the folk influence. The chorus is like a rallying cry, and the chord changes that slip in here and there bring a warmth to the sound.

Coulson slips in a wailing solo over the last 40 seconds, and the song fades... as does the band. This was the last Asia song on the last Asia album, and here's Wetton singing, 'Till we meet again, Think the best of me, Till we meet again'.

I'll admit that once John passed away in January 2017, this was the first song that popped into my mind, and I started to tear up a bit. Was this his elegy he was writing? Did he know he wouldn't be around much longer? He had serious health battles, so who knows. Either way, the song is sadly appropriate to the end of the band's recording career.

The final verse says it all:

Low expectation, but reach for the sky
True to yourself till the day you die
Stay safe and keep your powder dry
And don't drive any faster
Than your guardian angel can fly

With an excellent song like this on the album, it's surprising it was not played live.

Gravitas Rarities
'The Closer I Get to You' (acoustic) (Downes/Wetton)

While this version is slightly more tolerable than the album version, the song remains a lethargic listen. The sparse mix (which is just bass and drums removed) only emphasizes the unfortunate lyrics, and it's still over six minutes long. For a fan, it's definitely not worthy of being a bonus track. This was on the North American and European editions.

'Russian Dolls' (Acoustic) (Downes/Wetton)

Appearing on the Japanese release as a bonus cut, once again, we get very little differentiation from the original recording. Clearly, the band used up all the album material, as a result, the mildly different alternate-version bonus tracks are throwaways.

2014 And Beyond

The band toured to promote *Gravitas* in 2014 and then took a break as Wetton underwent cancer treatments, including chemotherapy.

In December 2016, it was announced Asia would be co-headlining with Journey on a North American jaunt scheduled to begin in March 2017. The band also announced a new live album would be on the way in 2017. Sadly, on 11 January 2017, it was announced that Wetton – needing chemotherapy again – would not be participating in the upcoming tour. Wetton hand-picked Billy Sherwood of Yes as his fill-in, which was rather eerie, as Chris Squire had bailed out of a co-headlining 2015 tour of Yes and Toto – to receive treatment for leukemia – and had also picked Sherwood (who had joined Yes in 1994 and again from 1997-2000) as his replacement. Squire passed away soon after, as would Wetton, on 31 January 2017.

Losing Wetton was devastating for the band, especially Downes. Sherwood is a fantastic bass player, but his voice was no match for Wetton's, and the band didn't sound right. Their hearts weren't in it anyway, and that was 100% understandable. After the tour, Downes continued with Yes, and Palmer busied himself with Carl Palmer's ELP Legacy tour. Coulson departed in 2018 and is now the guitarist for the Queen musical, *We Will Rock You*.

In the summer of 2019, Asia shockingly hit the road as part of a package tour with Yes, Carl Palmer's ELP Legacy, and a solo John Lodge of the Moody Blues. Downes, Palmer and Sherwood were joined by ex-Guns N' Roses member Ron 'Bumblefoot' Thal on guitars and vocals. Howe joined Asia onstage for the last four songs of their set each night.

While Thal is an excellent guitar player, his voice was decent but only average for Asia – further proof that they should have let things rest after Wetton's passing. Whether the 2016-2017 album-in-progress will ever be finished is unknown at this writing.

Asia Live Albums

This list will be a summary of Asia's officially released live albums. Neither official nor unauthorised bootlegs will be mentioned, but there are many of such things out there if you need to find them. The goal here is simply to mention the live album highlights, sound quality, performances, tracks of note, and personnel on said recordings.

Live in Moscow (1991)

Recorded in Moscow – in what was then the USSR – over two nights in November 1990, *Live in Moscow* was the first official live Asia album. Wetton, Downes and Palmer were all on board, with the new face being guitarist Pat Thrall: the first American to join the band.

Back in 1979, Elton John had been the first major act to play in the USSR, performing solo on piano with percussionist Ray Cooper. It wasn't until the summer of 1987 when the other piano man – Billy Joel – toured with a full band, that the Russian fans got a true concert experience from a foreign rock act. Over the next few years, Uriah Heep (they would sell-out ten straight shows to 180,000 fans in Moscow in December 1987), Black Sabbath, UB40, Scorpions and Yngwie Malmsteen would all follow, not to mention the massive Moscow Music Peace Festival concerts on 12 and 13 August 1989, with Ozzy Osbourne, Skid Row, Bon Jovi, Motley Crue, Cinderella and Scorpions.

By 1990, it was not exactly new for artists to play in the USSR, but it was still a great thing for Asia to do. *Live in Moscow* is a decent live album. The sound quality is quite good, although, at times, crowd noise is blatantly piped in, perhaps due to the fact that with Russian concert-goers usually being surrounded by armed military, they weren't exactly encouraged to rock out.

This tour was Asia's first since 1983. Thrall brought a heavy and rocking element to the group dynamic, which was what they wanted at that point in time. On songs like 'Time Again', 'Go', 'Rock And Roll Dream' and especially 'Sole Survivor', Thrall goes for broke come solo time. His frenetic attack on 'Sole Survivor' is exemplary and pretty jaw-dropping. But when it comes to the nuances of the more melodic material – such as 'Don't Cry', 'Only Time Will Tell' and 'Open Your Eyes' – Thrall seems a bit out of his element.

The drum solo on 'The Heat Goes On' is vintage Palmer and pretty top-notch, though it is badly edited down. Downes' keyboard instrumental piece mixes in a solo piece and a rendition of 'Video Killed The Radio Star'. Wetton gives a solo acoustic take on King Crimson's 'Book of Saturday' and there's an abridged version of that band's 'Starless' (if only it was all twelve minutes of the song). Thrall plays Robert Fripp's parts quite well. Pointlessly tacked on at the end is 'Kari-Anne': a 1987 Wetton/Downes song recorded with Gorham and Sturgis.

The *Live in Moscow* video features some songs that aren't on the album, as well as a lame video for 'Kari-Anne'. Also included was a video for a remix of 'Prayin' 4 A Miracle': shot on the cold streets of Moscow; it was interesting but had a low-budget look.

Now: Live in Nottingham (1999)

This album was part of a series of dodgy 'official bootlegs' and a release that the band later regretted approving. But it was from a professionally-recorded TV concert performed in Nottingham, UK on 23 June 1990. It features the Wetton/Downes/Palmer/Thrall lineup, and while they aren't exactly on fire, for a TV studio performance, it is rather good.

In some ways, it's better than *Live in Moscow*. It has thirteen songs and runs for around an hour. The inclusion of lesser-played songs (at the time) like 'Voice of America', 'Days Like These', 'Go' and 'Prayin' 4 A Miracle' is a nice surprise alongside the usual classics. Also, Palmer delivers a brief drum solo on 'The Heat Goes On'. 'Wildest Dreams' and 'Sole Survivor' open the show with aggressive back-to-back performances (especially from Thrall), 'The Smile Has Left Your Eyes' gets the full treatment, and 'Open Your Eyes' is fairly explosive as the finale.

America: Live in the USA (2003)

This double live CD was recorded at the Classic Rock Festival in Trenton, New Jersey, on 5 October 2002, and I was there. It is a complete show with the lineup of Downes/Payne/Govan/Slade, and is an outstanding performance. Unfortunately, the mix isn't all that great, with Govan's guitars sounding a bit thin, not enough bottom end on the drums, and the bass and keyboards are too loud at times.

The band played extremely well and were very up for the gig. It was also nice seeing Asia on a big stage again, even if the place was half empty (it was more crowded for the tremendous Uriah Heep set later that night). The set had nineteen songs, including vintage classics like the opener 'The Heat Goes On', 'Only Time Will Tell', 'Go', 'Sole Survivor', 'Days Like These', and of course, 'Heat Of The Moment'.

'Arena', 'Military Man' and 'Who Will Stop The Rain?' covered the Payne era, along with new *Aura* material 'Ready To Go Home', 'Wherever You Are', 'Kings Of The Day', and an explosive version of 'Free' where Govan blew the crowd away. There was also an acoustic set featuring three Payne-era songs and a Downes keyboard solo. Also included was a Govan instrumental piece, 'Bad Asteroid': a funky, jazz-fusion track with grooves and licks echoing some of the 1970s greats.

But the DVD of the show is not recommended. It looks low-budget, features interviews with the band and fans after each song, and suffers from sound issues. Also, a number of songs listed on the cover don't even appear. Classic Rock Productions were cranking out live CDs and DVDs from veteran prog acts like Asia, Uriah Heep and Nektar for a few years, and sometimes the quality suffered. Even the front cover looks like a bootleg.

It's a shame it was botched, but the Payne era was a constant struggle for respect, and this was no different. But don't let that overshadow a good performance.

Extended Versions (2007)

This budget-priced disc from Sony/BMG's strange *Extended Versions* series captured the band live in Helsinki, Finland, at the end of the 2005 *Silent Nation* tour. This series usually took live recordings from existing albums, but sometimes consumers actually got a new live album, as was the case here.

The sound quality and performances are very good. Ten songs appear, with seven from *Asia* and three from *Silent Nation*. It would've been nice to see a song or two from other albums, but what you got for the price was worthwhile for any Payne-era fan.

Fantasia: Live in Tokyo (2007)

Eagle Records here captured the 2006-2007 reunion tour, on both DVD and as a 2 CD set. The sold-out 2007 Japan tour accentuated how good the band sounds after more than 20 years apart.

The setlist is representative of what they played each night on the tour. Songs from only the *Asia* and *Alpha* albums were performed, and for the first time, songs from the band members' pasts. Thus we got 'Roundabout' by Yes (Howe), 'Fanfare For The Common Man' by ELP (Palmer), 'Video Killed The Radio Star' by The Buggles (Downes), and oddly, 'In The Court Of The Crimson King' by King Crimson (Wetton), a song originally featuring Greg Lake (and not Wetton) with Crimson. Everything sounded pretty good as far as the covers went, and the Buggles tune was especially light-hearted and fun with Wetton singing through a megaphone.

Additionally, Howe, Downes and Palmer took solo spotlights, and a few songs were done acoustically. The entire debut album was performed – though not consecutively – and the B-side, 'Ride Easy', was also played acoustically. Both the CD and DVD are well worth acquiring.

Spirit of the Night: The Phoenix Tour Live in Cambridge 2009 (2010)

Here we have a 2 CD/DVD set from the *Phoenix* tour, recorded in Cambridge, UK, in 2009 after the band had been on the road for about a year. The sound is excellent and the setlist has some changes from the previous tour.

A few new songs from *Phoenix* are a treat, with both 'Never Again' (a wonderful version) and 'An Extraordinary Life' sounding very good indeed. A real rarity is hearing 'My Own Time (I'll Do What I Want)' from *Alpha*, which sounds great (especially Howe's guitar work) and brings back fond memories.

There are also some wonderful bonuses. The CD includes both ELP's 'Fanfare For The Common Man' and the rarely played 'Midnight Sun' from a 2007 Detroit, Michigan show. The DVD omits those cuts but does add King Crimson's 'In The Court Of The Crimson King', recorded at the legendary Tower Theatre in Philadelphia, PA, with ex-Crimson member, Ian McDonald, on flute.

As for the DVD, it sounds wonderful and is mixed really well, but the footage goes more for an up-close and intimate feel, almost like an audience-shot show.

But it looks good – consider it a little piece of cinema vérité, if you will. This is another live set that is well worth your time.

Resonance: The Omega Tour Live in Basel 2010 (2012)

This may be my favourite of the Asia live releases. They really got everything right here, visually and sonically. The audio is excellent and the performance is strong. It looks so much better than the last release, plus it's a full show.

Quite a few tunes from the latest release at the time (*Omega*) appear, including the spirited opener 'I Believe', 'Holy War' (with Palmer's drum attack in the mid-section drawing an ovation), 'Finger On The Trigger', 'End Of The World', and the haunting 'Through My Veins', which is sublime. All the other songs have appeared before and still sound great, including the rocker, 'Go' (from *Astra*), which is a fan favourite, although Howe seems to struggle to inject anything heavy into it.

Palmer's drum solo and Howe's acoustic guitar segment (featuring 'All's A Chord' and 'The Valley Of Rocks') are also a big part of why this show was so excellent. Highly recommended.

High Voltage Live, 2010 (2014)

This recording saw the band at the UK's large High Voltage Festival back in 2010. The band played the whole debut album, although not in order. Also played were recent songs 'I Believe' and 'An Extraordinary Life'. This is a CD/DVD combo release and it can be hit and miss. Howe is not at his best here and flubs a few notes. Also, the backing vocals are off at times.

Otherwise, it's a decent show, but the sound isn't right. Make sure you do not get the bootleg 2 CD version (there's no need for two discs at all and that should be a warning right there) and go for the official release from Frontiers Records, who have handled all studio and live albums from Asia since 2008.

Axis XXX: Live In San Francisco MMXII (2015)

This show was aired on the popular cable music channel AXS TV in November 2012 and was released in 2015. As usual, it was a 2 CD/DVD combo release and was another very nice package. The playing is excellent, and the audio and video might be the best yet of any of the Frontiers live releases.

Opening with 'Only Time Will Tell' was a great idea, and, as always, there's an ample amount of tracks from the first two albums. The new album *XXX* is represented with sparkling takes on 'Face On The Bridge', 'Tomorrow The World' and a piano/vocal version of 'I Know How You Feel.' The acoustic segment goes on a little too long, but Howe plays his solo pieces – 'Pyramidology' and 'The Golden Mean' – with dexterity and skill.

This show was one of the last dates of the tour, and Howe would depart just a few months later – the end of the original reunion.

Besides supporting a new album in 2012, this also was the 30th anniversary of the debut album. Some fans griped that Howe didn't seem interested in his playing, but I do not see or hear that at all. His solos on 'Wildest Dreams' and 'Face on the Bridge' – not to mention the acoustic pieces – should be enough evidence that those claims are baseless. This is another highly-recommended live release.

Symfonia-Live in Bulgaria 2013 (2017)

This release was a special one, and not just because of the orchestral collaboration. Though it was recorded in 2013, it wasn't released until 2017, just a few months after John Wetton's passing.

They got it right with *Symfonia*. Recorded on 21 September 2013 in Plovdiv, Bulgaria, with the Plovdiv Opera Orchestra conducted by Levon Manukyan, this special one-off concert was well done considering the circumstances. The band only had a brief amount of time to meet and rehearse with the orchestra, but somehow it all came together in front of the TV cameras and the audience.

The concert was magnificent and wisely split into two parts, with the band playing seven songs alone and seven more with the orchestra. All the classic Wetton-era albums were represented, except for *Astra*, and the show flowed very well, the setlist carefully thought out.

The first set featured killer versions of 'Sole Survivor' (an inspired opening choice), 'Time Again', 'Face On The Bridge', 'My Own Time (I'll Do What I Want)', 'Holy War', 'An Extraordinary Life' and a fantastic rendition of 'Days Like These'. The band seemed to feed off new member Coulson and sounded particularly energized. His solos on 'Sole Survivor' and 'Time Again' blazed as he was ripped through some really impressive scales.

The orchestra joined in for the second set, which contained 'Open Your Eyes', 'Only Time Will Tell', 'Don't Cry', 'Heroine', 'The Smile Has Left Your Eyes', 'Wildest Dreams' and 'Heat Of The Moment'. The version of 'The Smile Has Left Your Eyes' was nothing short of tremendous. They did the extended two-part version with fiery power and beauty, and Coulson added a passionate and note-perfect solo. Wetton's voice cracked with emotion at the song's conclusion.

The crowd were very excited, although they are low in the mix and the cameras don't show them often enough. Another issue is with Palmer's camera, which zooms in and out a lot and is especially galling on Carl's solo during 'Wildest Dreams'.

The venue was Plovdiv's Roman Amphitheatre: an architectural marvel built over 2,000 years ago and an amazing setting for a concert.

Asia Odds And Ends

'Gypsy Soul' (Moroder/Whitlock)

Here is the oddest Asia song of them all, from the 1987 Sylvester Stallone movie, *Over The Top*. John Wetton actually sang the rocker 'Winner Takes It All' first, but the producers wanted a 'tougher' voice and instead got Sammy Hagar, who scored a hit with it. Wetton was then asked to sing 'Gypsy Soul', written by the soundtrack's producer, Oscar-winner, arranger and synthesizer player, Giorgio Moroder.

Moroder programmed drums and played keyboards on 'Gypsy Soul', accompanied by highly-respected session guitarist Dan Huff and Wetton on bass and vocals. Thus, Wetton is the only member of Asia on the track. Why this was listed as Asia is a complete mystery. Asia had split up by 1987, so a lot of fans were confused by this new song.

'Gypsy Soul' feels like typical 1980s soundtrack fodder. Huff's guitar solo is great, though, and Wetton's vocal performance is of note. The song was never played live and has never appeared on an Asia album.

'Did It All for Love' (M. Galley, T. Galley)

Also from 1987 is another off-track song: the Phenomena tune, 'Did It All For Love'. Phenomena were a studio-based hard rock project formed by ex-Whitesnake and Trapeze guitarist Mel Galley and his brother Tom. Their second album – *Phenomena II: Dream Runner* – featured John Wetton, who was asked to sing lead vocals on the song.

It's straight-up pop/rock, or AOR if you will, and in some ways could easily pass as an Asia song. It's got a fantastic chorus, and Wetton's voice slots in there perfectly. Also on the song were guitarists Mel Galley and Scott Gorham (the latter of Thin Lizzy); drummer Michael Sturgis, of A-ha; bassist Neil Murray, of Whitesnake; and the keyboard player, Leif Johansen, also of A-ha.

The video features the band with Wetton, and there are cameos from Max Bacon of GTR and Ray Gillen of Black Sabbath, who both also sang on the album. The video looks fantastic, with a mini-movie playing out behind the guys, some of it shot at Abbey Road Studios. The song became a minor hit in parts of Europe and Japan and even hit number one in Brazil for six weeks. The song was so huge there that Asia did an acoustic version of it when they played Brazil in 1991. This is just as much Asia as 'Gypsy Soul', if not more, with Gorham and Sturgis on it.

'Kari-Anne' (Downes/Wetton)

This 'new' studio song was added to the end of the *Live in Moscow* album, but it wasn't actually new. The song came from the 1987 sessions where the band nearly reformed with Downes, Wetton, ex-Thin Lizzy guitarist Scott Gorham, and former A-ha drummer, Michael Sturgis.

'Kari-Anne' is typical late-1980s pop/rock fare. It's not terrible but it is pretty subpar. The hooks aren't really all that memorable, and it only has a couple of sections. The opening guitar intro is classic Gorham, with some of that Thin Lizzy harmony guitar quality. The drumming sounds nothing like Palmer (it's Sturgis), and it's actually Francis Dunnery – formerly of It Bites and Robert Plant's band – who lays down the solos (which were recorded at a different time). The outro solo is actually pretty fiery and is the best part of the song. There's a lot of annoying late 1980s reverb on the track too.

The song had actually been played live in 1989, on some German dates that Wetton and Palmer did as a litmus test to see if Asia might be able to reform. John Young played keyboards and Holger Larisch was on guitar (a few dates in Europe supporting The Beach Boys had Alan Darby – formerly of the band Fashion – on guitar). There are fans who like this song because it's Wetton, but it's far below the quality of the first three albums.

'The Smile Has Left Your Eyes (Parts I & II)' (Newly Reconstructed Arrangement) (Wetton)

This was quite the surprise when it surfaced on 13 June 2020 on both Facebook and YouTube. It's a carefully reconstructed arrangement of the 1983 Asia gem. Rick Nelson – who was a friend and colleague of John Wetton – put this version together.

This is easily the most complete take on the song as it was originally conceived, and is of really good quality, making one wonder if a deluxe edition of *Alpha* with demos and outtakes could happen, because that stuff is out there. This version used parts of the demo and other takes and mixes, including what sound like monitor mixes. Nelson did a really nice job with this, and it sounded like quite a task. Nelson spoke of it on the official Asia website:

This track was painstakingly assembled from archival studio recordings of different reference mixes, each with relative levels out of context. Each tape had to be speed/time aligned to the best reference track available before attempting phase/cancel and mid/side mixing to extract a buried vocal or keyboard, for example, in order to mix the resulting track. In addition, each clip had to be EQ'd to match as closely as possible the released track, so it could dovetail into the only part of the released recording used on this track – the final end-tag. There are multiple edits and a lot of mixing of the various parts to counter overly loud or soft elements, all while ensuring drums/keyboards are aligned and not phasing. This involved many sections to keep each separate track from slightly drifting. While not perfect, it is the closest to the originally intended arrangement of the unfinished studio recordings.

If you're a die-hard Asia fan (and if you're reading this book, I assume you are), please seek this out!

Asia Compilation Albums

Then And Now (1990)
Highest Chart Positions: US: 114, Canada: 82, Japan: 39, Switzerland: 39

This was the first official Asia 'hits' package, and it was tied into the 1990 reunion of the band and released that summer. The idea was to feature old classics with new songs, but it didn't come off too well. Also, for some bizarre reason, the album was based on vinyl, with a short running time and two sides (side one was 'Then' and side two was 'Now'). By 1990, vinyl was virtually dead, so why this wasn't at least 60-70 minutes on CD is a total mystery. It came off as if it had little thought behind it, and being little more than a corporate decision by Geffen Records.

Three tracks from *Asia* were featured ('Heat of the Moment', 'Only Time Will Tell' and 'Wildest Dreams'), two from *Alpha* ('Don't Cry' and 'The Smile Has Left Your Eyes') and one from *Astra* ('Voice Of America'). Why the only hit from *Astra* ('Go') wasn't included makes no sense at all.

The cover illustration by Jean Francois-Podevin utilised the classic Roger Dean cover images: the Leviathan sea serpent from *Asia*, the eagle from *Alpha* and the female robot from *Astra*, accompanied by a Pegasus with a maze around them and the Earth above. It was a pretty sharp design. The 'new' songs are as follows:

'Days Like These' (Jones)
When Asia officially reunited and announced their comeback, they did so with this song that became an instant classic in the summer of 1990. 'Days Like These' is actually a cover of a song by Steve Jones (not the Sex Pistols guitarist), frontman for The Unforgiven.

Wetton described the song to reporter Pete Wolfe in 1990:

The demo was totally different from the track we've done, although the song is the same. When I first heard it, it didn't click. I thought this is weird for Asia to be doing something like this. Then I listened to it three times. When I went to bed that night, put my head on the pillow and turned the light out, the song was still going around in my head. I thought there must be something in this. After a couple of days, I really liked the song. So we went over to California and did the whole thing in two days with Steve Lukather of Toto playing guitar on it. It was absolutely wonderful.

Right from the opening chord, it sounds like classic Asia. The hallmarks are all there, with the bold synths, the melodic vocals, the inspirational chorus and the tight rhythms. And yet, it's not really Asia at all. As Wetton said, it's the legendary guitarist, Steve Lukather, of Toto. Session man, Jamie Green, plays the drums, and even though it sounds just like Downes on keyboards, it's actually Wetton.

The lyrics come off like stream-of-consciousness writing and are very unusual but quite inspirational. This was not easy for Wetton, but he nailed it. The chorus is as infectious as any of Asia's best songs, and producer Frank Wolf definitely got it right for this to sound like vintage Asia. Here's an example of how the lyrical approach:

The sun was shining and I was crying
I saw a thousand people singing in the rain
And I was thinking about the Indians
And how they say true wisdom only comes from pain
Come a rumbling, humbling feeling
Like things will never, ever be the same
But what doesn't kill you only makes you stronger
Today I'm strong enough, and anyway I love the rain

That's not easy at all to sing, let alone remember all that verbiage. Wetton stated earlier that he struggled with the idea of it at first but then came around, and how he made it work was wonderfully executed. Radio programmers certainly welcomed the band back, as this song soared all the way to number 2 on the Album Rock charts for three weeks. Even though it had burned up the radio since early August, Geffen Records didn't issue the single until mid-September. The music video had Wetton walking around a city in a business suit, ending up on top of a skyscraper. This was interspersed with clips of the band playing the song live from a UK TV appearance in June. For some unknown reason, the video was never submitted to MTV.

The single peaked at 64 on the US charts but would've easily cracked the Top 40 had the single been issued simultaneously with the rock radio release and the video been given the proper MTV support. But it did reach number 31 in Canada.

The CD single offered the album version, a single edit, and an 'AC Mix' for adult contemporary radio, which toned down the guitars and drums a bit. The actual single used 'Voice of America' as the B-side.

'Days Like These' is considered a classic by fans, for a good reason, and appears on every compilation of the original Asia. The song was prominently featured on the 1990-1991 *Then and Now* tour, but was not played again until the *Aura* tour of 2001-2002. After that, the original lineup welcomed it back on the 2010 *Omega* tour, the 2013 tour (Sam Coulson's first with the band), and the 2014 *Gravitas* tour.

'Prayin' 4 A Miracle' (Cassidy/Shifrin/Wetton)

Quite a few Asia fans were baffled at how 1970s teen heartthrob and *Partridge Family* star, David Cassidy, got involved in writing a song with the band. Wetton was friends with Sue Shifrin, who was Cassidy's wife at the time. Shifrin had written songs for other artists over the years, and she and Wetton decided to collaborate.

Wetton said this about the Cassidy collaboration in the Gallant book:

I'd written with his wife Sue Shifrin, over about the last three years. She's a songwriter who's based in L.A., and we have very similar tastes. We'd written about 10-12 songs together, and we were in California last year when she had an idea for a chorus that didn't have a verse. The three of us were sitting around the pool, and suddenly David and I hit on the idea of 'Prayin' 4 A Miracle'. It was sort of semi-autobiographical, if you like. We had some common ground there and before we knew it, the song was written.

Seeing as how both Cassidy and Wetton would have long-running battles with alcohol, it makes sense that they could bond over this idea of redemption after a struggle. The song itself is downbeat and opens with dark, moody keyboard chords before crunchy guitars and drums come in. Wetton sounds great, vocally. It's not that bad a song at all and is a bit of an earworm.

However, right down to the song's title with the number '4', and lines like 'I've been flat out of luck, Spent my very last buck, Can't sink no lower than this', it's hard not to wince a little, at the lyrics and how the song is geared to a different audience.

Producer Guy Roche plays drums, and the guitars are by session man, soundtrack composer and Cassidy guitarist Ron Komie. His solo on this track is pretty smokin', as he speedily flies through a bunch of notes with a flourish. Keyboard-wise, whether this is Downes or a session man is unknown.

A rare promo single with a totally different mix surfaced on the *Live in Moscow* video release. A music video filmed of the band playing on the streets of Moscow in the cold and snow, features this mix with heavier drums and guitars and almost sounds as if it's been slowed down.

This track was played live on the *Then and Now* tour, and with Palmer and Thrall able to add their own parts, it came off much, much better. After that tour, the song was never played live again.

Another song by Wetton, Cassidy and Shifrin from these 1990 writing sessions – titled 'I'll Never Stop Loving You' – ended up being covered by Heart, Cher and Cassidy himself.

'Am I In Love?' (Downes/Wetton)

An outtake from the *Astra* sessions, this is easily the most soft-rock song Asia ever recorded. Wetton was actually quite fond of it, and at the time of *Astra*'s *release* in 1985, he mentioned the song could end up on a solo album one day. Instead, five years later, it ended up on *Then and Now*.

The track is largely built around ultra-light keyboard chords, a lilting chorus, and not much else. The chorus of 'Am I in Love?' is uttered many, many times thus there's no confusion as to the song's title. Wetton's vocals are fine, and Palmer's drums are prominent (but with far too much reverb), so it's not all a loss. Mandy Meyer is virtually invisible, appearing only for a few notes where a solo would typically be.

The keyboards are awash with lushness, the synth strings are syrupy, and there is no variation in sound. On the bridge, Downes brings in some of his classic embellishments, and Wetton has a few bass notes that prop things up, but it's a long way from 'Sole Survivor' to say the least.

'Summer (Can't Last Too Long)' (Downes/Wetton)

This was another recording from the 1987 Gorham and Sturgis sessions. It's a catchy, straight-up pop/rock song. With the album having been released in summer, this song's inclusion was well-timed.

Pumping synths and handclaps percolate throughout the tune, dating it instantly. There's a simple approach, accentuating the pop aspect. The band is not trying to write a rock opera here, and that's fine. The choruses are alive with thick guitar power chords, hard-rocking drums and great hooks. The problem is the lyrics, which lack substance. Not every song needs to be award-winning, and this one sure isn't: 'Summer can't last too long, Summer can't last too long, Spring, winter or fall, But out of them all, Summer can't last too long'.

It's a fun, harmless song, all the better for a nice Scott Gorham guitar solo, although some of the notes are buried in the noisy mix. It would've been cool to see this lineup do an album, but the record industry – apart from that of Japan – had no interest, so it didn't happen.

Then and Now would only reach 114 in the US charts, but it sold steadily through the years, eventually going gold. Again, the band botched a US tour. After cancelling the second leg of 1983's *Asian Invasion Tour* and then cancelling the whole 1985 *Astra* tour, the band had a chance to win back US audiences but failed to do so. In 1990, there were two co-headlining tour possibilities – with either Fleetwood Mac or the Moody Blues – but both fell through due to bad management decisions. Aside from an appearance on the syndicated radio program, *Rockline* (where they also played a few songs acoustically in the studio), they did no promotion in North America.

Though Pat Thrall got the job on guitar, Asia had reached out to someone else first. That was brilliant Canadian guitarist/vocalist/writer, Rik Emmett of Triumph (who can play hard rock, heavy metal, jazz, flamenco, classical, blues, progressive rock and just about anything else). In 2015 I interviewed Emmett for my book *Unstrung Heroes: Fifty Guitar Greats You Should Know*, and we were talking about some players he really liked. He mentioned Elliot Randall for his work in Steely Dan, and that led to him telling an interesting tale. Our chat was nearly two hours long, so I'll pick it up from the snippet where we got onto the subject of Asia.

Rik: I sometimes do cover gigs just for fun and I had to learn 'Reelin' in the Years' by Steely Dan, and that solo is crazy by Elliot Randall. Holy shit, is that ever

a great solo! There's another guitar player that people should know about. The lead guitar parts are so clever and tricky. That's another guy under the radar.
Me: I think he's brilliant. He was even in Asia for a while in the late 90s.
Rik: Was he? I did not know that.
Me: Well, it wasn't the classic lineup, but he was a part of the band led by Geoff Downes and John Payne.
Rik: You know, they pitched to me at one point.
Me: Asia? Is that true?
Rik: Yeah, it was. They only had a few European festivals on the books, but Steve Howe wasn't there, and I got calls from both Carl Palmer and John Wetton. And I heard these very cultivated British voices on the phone saying [does decent British accent], 'I think it would be really fantastic if you joined the group, you'd be the perfect guy'. I had to pass though, as there weren't enough gigs to put in all that work.
Me: This must've been in 1990 when three of the four from the original lineup reformed and released Then and Now.
Rik: Yes, that's exactly when that was.
Me: They ended up choosing Pat Thrall.
Rik: Did they? He was a good choice.

So there you go, some fascinating information, right from the man himself. Rik actually would've been a dynamite fit with Asia, as he'd have been able to do the electric and acoustic parts. Plus, there's his superlative voice. But at that point, the band only had about five or six shows lined up and he couldn't commit.

Archiva 1 (1996) / Archiva 2 (1996)

These two compilations mentioned earlier in the book were collections of demos, unfinished ideas, B-sides, unreleased tracks and rarities from the John Payne era – although some were demos Payne did before he joined the band.

It's very hit and miss: there's some gold and some garbage. Of the Volume 1 tracks not already mentioned, the best would be 'The Boys From Diamond City'. This lively rocker originated from the 1987 Wetton/Downes/Gorham/Sturgis recordings and was finished off in 1988 with Payne on vocals. The song is an anthemic rocker that starts with a sweet keyboard intro. Then chiming guitars and pounding drums and bass come in, and the song lifts to a new height. Payne sounds great and doesn't overdo things at all. The verses and pre-chorus are dynamic. Then the crunchy guitars, keyboard lines, drums and bass fills accompany the vocals on the main chorus and it all coheres. Gorham gets in a great solo, and then wistful keyboards suddenly appear on their own, with gorgeous harmony vocals floating in before the rocking starts anew. This is the only track not previously mentioned that's really a standout.

'Tears' was a demo of a pretty decent song that would later surface on Geoff's 1992 solo album, *Vox Humana*, with ex-GTR singer Max Bacon, on vocals. 'A.L.O.' was a wretched attempt at an ELO spoof that should never have been released for public consumption, and 'I Believe' was a 1987 demo (with bad drum machine) by Payne and Andy Nye that is unintentional comedy. 'Dusty Road' started as an instrumental Downes work that Bacon wrote lyrics for, and Payne later added vocals to. This track could've been something if developed further.

As for the unmentioned *Archiva 2* tracks, 'Moon Under The Water' and 'Satellite Blues' are demos from 1988 that would be reworked for *Vox Humana*. Neither are particularly good, but 'Satellite Blues' was a semi-gritty rocker. Another Payne/Nye demo from 1987, called 'Love Like The Video', is pretty awful, as you'd expect from that title. 'Can't Tell These Walls' is about the same, and 'The Higher You Climb' isn't so hot either. That track originally had Max Bacon on vocals, but it is Payne on this recording. 'Armenia' was originally for a 1990 benefit album and was touched up in 1996.

Overall, you will find some good things and some bad things. Think of it as a yard sale where you know there's a lot of junk sitting there, but if you're willing to sift through, you'll find those treasures.

Anthology (1997)

This release was another doomed project from the Payne era. Timed to coincide with the band's 15th anniversary, a tour was planned, but ultimately scrapped when the album wasn't even issued in North America. Snapper Records couldn't get the rights to the Geffen material, so the band re-recorded five classics from *Asia*, *Alpha* and *Astra*. They added two new songs and selected songs from *Aqua*, *Aria* and *Arena*.

The whole thing was kind of a mess, and Payne later expressed regret about the re-recordings. Many artists do re-records for licensing purposes for TV, films and commercials, but these were done solely to get the songs on the compilation. Here's a look at the new material.

'The Hunter' (Downes)

This song was originally by another 1980s progressive rock supergroup, known as GTR, which included Steve Howe and ex-Genesis guitarist Steve Hackett, not to mention singer Max Bacon, formerly of Bronz and Nightwing. 'The Hunter' was a minor hit single and scored significant Album Rock airplay in the US and was an MTV exclusive video that summer of 1986.

There are lots of connections here: Howe had of course been an Asia member, and the GTR album was produced by Downes, who also wrote 'The Hunter'. Hackett had produced a Nightwing song sung by Bacon, and Nightwing's album cover for 1984's *My Kingdom Come* was designed by Roger Dean of Yes and Asia fame. Additionally, Brian Lane managed GTR, just as he had both Yes and Asia

However, this version sounds like a home demo. Payne's funky guitar riffs don't work, and he doesn't come close to Bacon's original vocal, which was a stunning performance.

'The Hunter' is an emotional masterpiece, but this version lacked all drama and was a disappointing take on a great song.

'Different Worlds' (Downes/Payne)

This was a newly-written song. Clocking in at around six minutes or so, it was pretty decent and mysterious-sounding. It has a lot of the touches from *Arena* and is a fairly mellow number, and it should do you well if you like the Payne material. Not a whole lot of variation occurs, but it's a cut that works fairly well within the Payne-era sound and wouldn't have been a bad track for any of the last few albums.

'Heat Of The Moment'/'Only Time Will Tell'/'Don't Cry/'The Heat Goes On'/'Go'/'Time Again'

These songs were re-recorded because the rights to the original recordings could not be acquired from Geffen Records. The only way to get these songs on this compilation was to re-record them. It wasn't a good idea.

Each song is a pale imitation of the original, with a flat, dry mix and awkward reverb usage. Not one of these re-recordings is worthy. 'Time Again' was a bonus track, and is an acoustic version that at least attempts something different. Even Downes and Payne acknowledged that this didn't turn out very well. Incidentally, I had the first pressing, which included the original versions of 'Heat Of The Moment' and 'Only Time Will Tell'. But that version was pulled from the shelves due to legal issues. Stay away from these re-recordings unless you're curious.

Rare (1999)

Calling this Asia is a serious stretch, so I'll be brief. It's a collection of recordings Downes and Payne did for the BBC nature documentary, *Salmon: Against the Tides*, and also a CD-ROM video game for Sony that never got released. The documentary music is just snippets running from 30 seconds to three minutes. The longer pieces – for the video game – are in the three to the four-minute range.

The style is a mix of new age and symphonic pop, and everything is instrumental. The Downes pieces for the documentary are nice - right up his alley. Some of that music echos latter-day Tangerine Dream or Kitaro. It's not bad at all and is a relaxing listen. But the video game music has some pretty awful attempts at techno, industrial rock and Harold Faltermeyer-style soundtrack music. However, this is not an Asia album in the least, despite the label slapping the name on there. start here

The Very Best of Asia: Heat of the Moment (1982-1990) (2000)

This was the first worthy Asia compilation and it was extremely well put together. Finally, Geffen/Universal remembered Asia had been on the label, and here was a compilation stacked with nearly 80 minutes of music from the first four albums.

We get six tracks from *Asia*, five from *Alpha*, three from *Astra* and one from *Then and Now*: the big kicker being the addition of the three rare B-sides (rare at the time anyway), 'Ride Easy', 'Daylight' and 'Lying To Yourself.' Liner notes and chart information were also provided for each track. It was a quality remaster, the only blemishes being they were the single edits of 'Sole Survivor' and 'Here Comes the Feeling', and the cover design by the studio Vartan was questionable. Aside from those details, this is what compilation albums should be like.

Anthologia-The 20th Anniversary-Geffen Years Collection (1982-1990) (2002)

You couldn't ask for much more from a compilation than what this double CD set provides. Included in their entirety are all three of the classic studio albums, the four new songs from *Then and Now* and the three B-sides from the *Heat of the Moment* compilation from two years earlier. Everything from the Geffen years is here except for one or two obscurities. The remastering is equal in quality to the last compilation and the liner notes are good. The cover art is nothing great, but as far as the content goes, this one is pretty amazing. In 2005 it would be reissued as *Gold*: remastered, with a vintage 1982 photo on the cover.

20th Century Masters-The Millennium Collection: The Best of Asia (2003)

This release was part of Universal's budget-priced Millennium Collection series that were usually limited to around eleven or twelev songs. This one fails. It included only three songs from the debut album, which is mind-boggling. These compilations were aimed at the casual music consumer, therefore making this one nonessential.

The Definitive Collection (2006)

Highest Chart Positions: US: 183

This high quality compilation was tied into Asia's reunion tour of late summer 2006. All tracks are full-length and newly remastered, significantly louder. Some may not like to hear the songs this way, but I feel it's nice to hear them with so much punch.

There are five songs from *Asia*, four from *Alpha*, three from *Astra,* one from *Then and Now*, plus the B-side 'Daylight', and the ultra-rare UK 12" mix of 'Go' (reviewed earlier in the *Astra* rarities section).

The US retailer, Best Buy, issued an exclusive edition including a DVD featuring the videos for 'Heat of the Moment', 'Only Time Will Tell', 'Wildest

Dreams', 'Don't Cry', 'The Smile Has Left Your Eyes' and 'Go'. This edition is now deleted, but any Asia fan should seek out a copy. The liner notes are brief but acceptable, and the chart information is accurate. *The Definitive Collection* would be the first Asia album to reach the US charts in sixteen years.

Heat of the Moment: Essential Collection (2013)

This UK-only release was from the Universal compilation arm known as Spectrum. The Spectrum releases are noted for their low price and generous song amounts. But the included tracks are often haphazardly chosen, and such is the case here.

We get five from *Asia*, five from *Alpha*, and a whopping six from *Astra*, along with the obligatory one from *Then and Now*. Among the oddball choices are 'True Colors', 'The Last To Know', 'After The War', 'Countdown To Zero', 'Hard On Me' and 'Rock And Roll Dream'. It's nice but strange to see all those on here. The B-side, 'Daylight', also appears. Also, the tracks are not in chronological order, which becomes jarring.

The cover utilises Roger Dean's artwork (though it's not a new design), making this the only Asia compilation to use Dean's visuals aside from *Then and Now*.

Asia Video Releases

This is a short look at the significant Asia video releases that haven't already been discussed in the live albums section. The live CD/DVD combo releases from 2007-2017 will not be repeated here. Track listings will be included for these releases.

Asia in Asia (1984)

Tracklist: 'The Heat Goes On'/'Here Comes The Feeling'/'Eye To Eye'/'Sketches In The Sun'/ (Steve Howe acoustic solo)/'Only Time Will Tell'/'Open Your Eyes'/(Geoff Downes keyboard solo)/'The Smile Has Left Your Eyes'/'Wildest Dreams'/(Carl Palmer drum solo)/'Heat Of The Moment'/'Sole Survivor.'

This was a 1984 Vestron Video VHS release of the infamous 6 December 1983 concert, broadcast on MTV and the Westwood One radio network, live-to-air via satellite from Tokyo's Budokan. At the time, this was the largest satellite event ever, having an audience of over 20 million.

Bassist/vocalist, Greg Lake (ex-King Crimson, ELP), replaced John Wetton, and on paper, it made sense. Lake had played for a decade with Palmer in ELP and had always had a knack for pop/rock songs. The gig – set up months in advance – was billed as *Asia in Asia*. On show night, there was an MTV-sponsored contest tied in, and the network broadcast a documentary titled *The Road to Budokan.*

Lake performed honourably, thought the need to fit his voice around Wetton's, sounded off at times. Lake also had to read a lot of the lyrics from a teleprompter – as he was only just learning the songs – but he did well under the circumstances. Additionally, the songs had been transposed down at least a minor-third and didn't always sound right. Palmer was less than thrilled, and Howe and Downes knew it. It was good, but not good enough. Still, this and the four other Japanese concerts had few, if any, errors.

Songs performed that night but not included in the video were 'Time Again', 'Cutting It Fine' and 'Daylight'. Later on, on the Japanese tour, they added 'Don't Cry'.

The Vestron Video package showed little knowledge of the product inside. The opener 'Time Again' was incorrectly listed as 'Time And Time Again', and the song was not even on there! 'Here Comes The Feeling' was also incorrectly listed, as 'Here Comes That Feeling'.

In an interview on *vintagerock.com*, Lake discussed joining the band in late 1983:

What happened was, I got a call one night from Carl Palmer, and he said, 'Greg, can you do me a favour?'. I thought he wanted to borrow a guitar or something, so I said, 'Yeah, of course, what do you want?'. He said, 'Aw man, we've fallen out with John, the lead singer and we've committed to do this satellite broadcast in Japan', and I said, 'Yeah?'. He said, 'Well, also MTV has run this huge competition where they're flying the prize winners over on a specially chartered 747. There's no backing out of it. They've paid for all the planes and everything'. So I said again, 'Yeah?'. He said, 'Could you come to do that one show?'. There were actually four shows. He then asked, 'Can you cover for him?'. I said, 'I don't know all the songs, Carl'. He said, 'Well, you can learn them'. So I asked, 'When is it?'. He said, 'Ten days'. I said, 'No, I can't do that', and he said, 'Aw, man'. Then I got a call from David Geffen, and to be quite honest, they offered me so much money, there was no way I could refuse it. And so, I did it. I sat up day and night with the lyrics. When it came to showtime, I had a lyric prompter, and I did it. To learn someone's entire set, and all the nuances, all the cues and all the little points, to remember all the chord shifts and make the lyrics sound the same as the record – it was a severe undertaking. I wouldn't want to do it again.

This concert has never been officially issued on DVD, though there are some (atrocious) bootlegs of it out there. But there are great soundboard and FM recordings of the show: I have those and definitely recommend hearing them. Greg Lake did a really good job under insane circumstances. This was a weird time in Asia's history.

Andromeda: Live in the UK '90 (1990)
Tracklist: 'Wildest Dreams'/'Sole Survivor'/'Don't Cry'/'Voice Of America'/'Time Again'/'Prayin' 4 A Miracle'/'The Smile Has Left Your Eyes'/'Only Time Will Tell'/'Days Like These'/'The Heat Goes On'/(Drum solo)/'Go'/'Heat Of The Moment'/'Open Your Eyes'

The tracklist is the same as the *Now: Live in Nottingham* CD included in the live albums section. This concert filmed in Nottingham, UK, in front of a small TV studio audience, was released on VHS home video and LaserDisc. The gig was one of Asia's first since reforming in 1990 (in fact, their second performance, following a festival appearance in Germany, where Wetton had a sore throat). The lineup was Wetton/Downes/Palmer/Thrall, and they sound very good considering the TV studio environment.

This release has seen numerous reissues on different labels, with different titles over the years, some of them rather shoddy.

Live in Moscow (1991)
Tracklist: 'Only Time Will Tell'/'Sole Survivor'/(Keyboard solo)/'Days Like These'/'Rendezvous 6.02'/'The Heat Goes On'/(Drum solo)/'Book Of Saturday'/'Prayin' 4 A Miracle' (Music video, not live)/'Go'/'The Smile Has Left Your Eyes'/'Open Your Eyes'/'Heat Of The Moment'/'Kari-Anne' (Music video, not live)

The video version of *Live in Moscow* differs greatly from the CD. The tracks exclusive to the video are 'Days Like These', a cover of the UK song 'Rendezvous 6.02', a different Downes keyboard solo, and the music videos for 'Prayin' 4 A Miracle' and 'Kari-Anne.' The video quality is pretty good, but nothing exceptional. Wetton plays some bum notes that are more obvious on the video than the CD, and he doesn't seem to be all that enthused. Perhaps he knew he wouldn't be a part of the band again soon.

This video was initially issued by Rhino Records in 1991 and has seen many different DVD releases, some legitimate and others of abysmal quality. Make sure you get the official release.

Asia Members In Spin-off Bands

I wanted to make sure to cover albums by significant post-Asia groups the members recorded with, such as iCon (Wetton and Downes), GTR (Howe with Downes producing), Ride The Tiger (Lake and Downes), 3 (Palmer), and Carl's pre-Asia project: PM, which I can't imagine too many people have written about until now.

iCon albums
iCon (2005)
Personnel:
John Wetton: bass, vocals, classical and acoustic guitars
Geoff Downes: keyboards, vocoder
John Mitchell: guitars
Steve Christey: drums
Hugh McDowell: cello
Released: 2 August 2005
Producers: John Wetton, Geoff Downes

In 2005, Wetton and Downes teamed up and, using a backing band, began releasing albums as iCon. There were similarities to Asia, but for the most part, it was a different, more mellow animal.

Asia fans were really pleased that John and Geoff were not just talking and working again but also recording. This music differs from Asia stylistically, having more choral moments and dreamy keyboards and atmospherics, with an almost spiritual feel. The sound is also somewhat orchestral.

Guitars are there, but take a back seat to the keyboards, vocals and cello of ex-ELO member Hugh McDowell. Among the best cuts are 'God Walks With Us', 'Let Me Go', 'Please Change Your Mind' and 'Spread Your Wings'. Keep in mind, this is quite mellow and wispy, and at times the songs blend, sounding the same. This was music to relax to and take in, not rock out with. It was great to have the guys back together, and clearly, the vibe was good, leading to the Asia reunion the following year.

iCon II: Rubicon (2006)
Personnel:
John Wetton: bass, vocals, classical and acoustic guitars
Geoff Downes: keyboards, vocoder
John Mitchell: guitars
Steve Christey: drums
Hugh McDowell: cello
Additional musicians: Anneke van Giersbergen (vocals on two tracks), Katie Jacoby (violin on two tracks)
Released: 10 November 2006

Producers: John Wetton, Geoff Downes

Wetton and Downes returned in 2006 with another iCon album, titled *Rubicon*. The title track is another spiritual song and a real triumph that would be suited for use in a feel-good movie. This album is mellow like the iCon debut. Few tracks up the tempo, but one that does is the rocker, 'Finger On The Trigger', which Asia would later rework for the *Omega* album.

'The Die Is Cast' is a great opener. It's mellow but quickly becomes a pulsating 1980s synth-laced pop/rock song. The keyboards may sound dated, but it's a good song. 'Reflections (Of My Life)' – a pensive song that reminisces and looks back at past mistakes – is a moving piece of music.

'The Hanging Tree' has percussion in support of a ghostly orchestral feel. Coincidentally, Uriah Heep had a great song called 'The Hanging Tree' on their album recorded after Wetton left, but it bears no resemblance to this song. Bottom line: If you enjoyed the first iCon album, you'll like this one better.

iCon 3 (2009)
Personnel:
John Wetton: bass, vocals, classical and acoustic guitars
Geoff Downes: keyboards, vocoder
Dave Kilminster: guitars
Peter Riley: drums
Hugh McDowell: cello
Additional musicians: Ann-Marie Helder (vocals on two tracks), Andreas Vollenweider (harp on two tracks)
Released: 13 March 2009
Producers: John Wetton, Geoff Downes

Somehow, in 2009, Wetton and Downes found time for a third iCon album. There are a couple of upbeat pop/rockers, like 'Twice The Man I Was' and 'Sex, Power And Money' (the latter having plenty of power chords and almost sounding like Spinal Tap in the chorus). 'Don't Go Out Tonight' is perky enough, but it's just not that good: the synths sound dated, and the lyrics are really odd (is this really about staying in for the night and watching TV?).

There are plenty of mushy orchestral-sounding ballads, and like the first two albums, things all start to blend in. But then there's the excellent 'Green Lights And Blue Skies', which sees Geoff using vocoder sounding as if right out of the ELO classic, 'Mr. Blue Sky'. I'd describe this as a sort of cheeky homage; after all, ex-ELO member, Hugh McDowell, is on the album. Additionally, David Kilminster contributes a squealing guitar solo. This ends up as a fun song.

'My Life Is In Your Hands' is a slow-building six-and-a-half-minute epic with excellent Wetton vocals and a great guitar solo from Kilminster. It's a well-structured song that sets an intriguing mood.

'Never Thought I'd See You Again' is a pretty, musical moment. A flighty keyboard fill accompanies Wetton's simple vocal, and when things lift up, it becomes a genuinely inspired pop song. This song is worthy of many from the Asia reunion albums, and it deserves to be covered and made into the smash it should've been. McDowell adds nice cello touches, and again, Kilminster is splendid on guitar, being a crucial iCon addition.

I interviewed Kilminster for my book, *Unstrung Heroes,* and we briefly talked about his time playing with guys like Keith Emerson, Carl Palmer and John Wetton:

Well, I guess John gave me my first break, so I'll always be thankful to him for that, and it was very cool to be able to play hit singles from Asia, technically challenging pieces from UK, and prog epics like King Crimson all during the same gig! And through playing with John and Carl Palmer in a band called Qango, I got to meet one of my musical heroes in Keith Emerson! That was such an amazing time, playing music that I grew up listening to. I managed to talk Keith into doing the whole of 'Tarkus' as well, all twenty minutes of it! And to play those pieces live, listening to Keith just wailing on the Moog or the Hammond, along with my favourite rhythm section ever, it was just heaven.

Although not all of *iCon 3* is great, it's still a worthy listen, and all the iCon albums have more than enough to satisfy fans of the Wetton/Downes writing team. However, these albums are largely a mellow affair, with modest production and arrangements. The material is good, but not at all the same as Asia.

There was also a November 2017 release titled *iCon Zero*, that was a simple repackaging of the 2002 *Wetton-Downes* demos album, with three bonus tracks: 'Oh! Carolann', (basically the exact same song as 'Kari-Anne'), 'She Knows', and an alternate version of 'I Would Die for You'. Incidentally, the original version of 'Kari-Anne' (from *Live in Moscow)* also appears here.

Most of the other songs from *Wetton-Downes* date from 1987 to 1989 or so, when Asia was defunct. 'We Move As One' – written during the *Astra* sessions – ended up being given to Abba's Agnetha Faltskog in 1985 and is included here in its actual form from her album, *Eyes of a Woman*. It's a nice enough song, but in the adult contemporary vein, and it made sense that Asia did not record it.

'Please' is a pretty song on the conventional subject of heartbreak and could've been developed into a big production number. 'Soul' is an instrumental that sounds similar to Jan Hammer's TV music for *Miami Vice* – or any other 1980s cop show for that matter – but it is interesting.

'Walking On Air' is a very good song, too, though not much else stands out on here. But it is a treat hearing the early demo of 'Summer (Can't Last Too Long)', a song which ended up on 1990's *Then and Now*.

Above and below: Geoff Downes and John Wetton onstage with Icon in early 2006, just months before the original line up of Asia reformed. (*Stephen Lambe*)

GTR Albums
GTR (1986)
Personnel:
Steve Howe: acoustic and electric guitars, guitar synthesizers, backing vocals
Steve Hackett: acoustic and electric guitars, guitar synthesizers, backing vocals
Max Bacon: lead vocals
Phil Spalding: bass, backing vocals
Jonathan Mover: drums, percussion
Released: 29 April 1986
Recorded: The Townhouse (London, UK) 1985-86
Producer: Geoff Downes
Engineer: Alan Douglas
Cover Illustration: Ian Miller
Highest Chart Position: US: 11, UK: 41

Following his unhappy departure from Asia in the fall of 1984, Steve Howe was looking for a new musical experience. Brian Lane – who managed Steve in both Yes and Asia – introduced him to ex-Genesis guitarist Steve Hackett, who was also looking for something new after his successful solo career had started to falter. A few weeks later, Howe and Hackett agreed to meet, deciding that if they couldn't write anything worthy on the first day, they would not pursue a new project.

That first meeting proved fruitful, so it was time to form a band. Though largely unknown, the players chosen were top-notch. Bassist, Phil Spalding, had played with Mike Oldfield, and drummer, Jonathan Mover, had been with Marillion for a short time. Rounding out the band was vocalist Max Bacon, who had been with Nightwing and Bronz. It was when Hackett produced a track on the 1984 Nightwing album *My Kingdom Come*, that he met Bacon and was impressed with the singer's outstanding alto/tenor vocal range.

Initially, GTR attracted little interest, although Geffen looked like they might sign the band. Ultimately, Clive Davis inked an Arista Records deal with the group. From the start, Hackett had misgivings over Lane's managing style and the wasting of money, but musically, things went very well.

Geoff Downes was selected as the producer. At the time, Hackett commented on the choosing of Downes in an interview with *Billboard Magazine*: 'We wanted to have a synthesizer brain. We wanted to be able to plug into his brain cells basically, but without having his hands there doing the playing. We wanted to trigger it via fretboard, as opposed to the keyboard'.

The idea was to use guitar synthesizers rather than actual synths and make the album as guitar-based as possible. But critics were scathing of the album, which was no surprise at all. To this day, progressive rock fans have polar opinions of the album. In this author's opinion, *GTR* is excellent from start to finish.

Released in the spring of 1986 (not in July as is commonly stated online incorrectly), *GTR* performed very well indeed, narrowly missing the Top 10 on the US album charts. But the album went gold, spawning a smash in the soaring 'When The Heart Rules The Mind', which hit number 14 on the US singles chart, going all the way to number 3 at Album Rock (though in the UK the song only reached 82 on the singles chart). Also, the video was an MTV Top 20 request item for several weeks. The song has a variety of segments and memorable hooks and boasts an outstanding performance from Bacon, demonstrating his high vocal range. The guitars and guitar synths blend well, and there are even some nice classical guitar parts in the bridge.

A follow-up single – 'The Hunter' – was issued in the summer. Written by Downes, it's a masterpiece, and Bacon's performance is downright spine-tingling. The lyrics are spiritual and thought-provoking, and the atmosphere crafted is sublime. The single stalled at 85 in the US, but the song did rise to 14 at Album Rock. It also received an MTV exclusive for its classy video. This song is one of Downes' best compositions, hands down, and Bacon's lyric interpretation is exactly what the song required.

Later that summer, Howe, Hackett and Bacon appeared on MTV's Guest VJ Hour, picking their favourite videos while hanging out at a New York guitar shop. MTV also broadcast a documentary about the making of the album.

The tracks 'Jekyll And Hyde', 'Here I Wait', 'You Can Still Get Through' and 'Reach Out (Never Say No)', are melodic-based rock songs with progressive touches and a heavier sound than Asia. 'Toe The Line' has a pretty melody and takes advantage of Bacon's voice. 'Imagining' is a great album closer, featuring Howe and Hackett's incredible acoustic interplay.

Two instrumentals adorn the album. One is Howe's tranquil 'Sketches In The Sun', which he premiered acoustically at the *Asia in Asia* concert in Japan in late 1983, although it is here played on 12-string electric guitar. The piece maintains its beauty on electric, and in fact, might be even more soothing. This is a testament to Steve's writing skills.

Steve Hackett took the opposite route for his instrumental piece, 'Hackett To Bits.' This track, which is effectively a reworking of his solo piece 'Please Don't Touch', is a hammering assault on the senses, with metallic, angular guitars and wailing noises sounding like something King Crimson's Robert Fripp might've written. It works extremely well, Hackett adding tremolo and fast runs that Eddie Van Halen would've been envious of. Mover and Spalding supply a rhythmic attack of heavy floor toms and some slapping/popping bass, respectively.

Hackett had bad feelings about the financial situation and called a meeting, voicing his concerns. Deciding to stay no longer, he departed in 1987. Later on, Hackett had this to say on MTV:

I always felt that something like GTR had novelty value. As soon as people start mentioning the word 'supergroup', it basically has novelty for one album. I suspect that no one was really all that surprised that Steve and I – although we are very good friends these days – didn't ride off into the sunset together, making albums for infinity.

Interviewing Hackett in 2015 for my book, *Unstrung Heroes,* we only touched slightly on the subject of GTR, but he did say, 'I enjoyed recording the material and the shows were fun too. We were thrilled it took off so well in the States'.

After Hackett left and Mover joined Joe Satriani's band, Howe opted to keep GTR going, adding guitarist/vocalist Robert Berry, from the obscure progressive band Hush, and ex-Saxon drummer, Nigel Glockler (who would later record on the *Aqua* sessions). Geoff Downes produced the demos in 1987 and recalled this on *vintagerock.com*:

I produced that one as well. We were about two-thirds of the way through the album and Arista Records was not happy with the direction the band was taking. They weren't thrilled with the idea that a group called GTR had only one featured guitarist as such. Robert Berry came in and Jonathan Mover had left. Arista indicated that unless the band came up with a lineup that they would be interested in, they wouldn't fund them anymore. At that point, I wanted to leave. I had my own things to do. I didn't want to watch the band on its knees.

I asked Howe about this time in our interview from 2001, and he was fairly dismissive about any 'second album' that was being made:

Well, there's a lot of nonsense and utter drivel about the second recording. There are actually two further recordings after GTR, both done without Steve Hackett, so they were never really destined to be called GTR because GTR was only a group with Steve Hackett and I in it. So at that point, yeah, I went off with the guys and we broke ties with Steve Hackett. Well, we invited Steve Hackett to come with us, but he didn't want to, so that was the breaking of the ties there. So we went to my studio in the country and we did some tracks, which are not going to surface unless I decide to release them. Then, with Arista's blessing, we went into the studio and started recording another whole bunch of music. And it was during that period that the drawbridge went up permanently on that project, when the new member – who was Robert Berry – through either his own desire or through mismanagement, ended up joining or going, to make the group 3.

I asked Steve if any of this material would surface one day, or if it was even worthy of public consumption:

That left the new GTR really high and dry, and Arista pulled the plug. And the tapes have been buried, and sadly the tapes aren't really worth wanting to hear because they were really, in the true sense of the word, backing tracks. These were very simplistic recorders we used. After that, there was nothing. So, both the Arista tapes were not suitable for release. And my tapes are suitable for release, and maybe at some point they're going to be released through my own goals, for my own reasons, you know, because Max... Max Bacon and I are still good friends and really, the tapes we did were very much about Max and I.

The King Biscuit Flower Hour Presents GTR (1997)

In 1997, the popular radio concert series, *The King Biscuit Flower Hour,* issued from its archives a GTR show recorded at Los Angeles' Wiltern Theatre on 19 July 1986. The show was broadcast later that summer, and I distinctly remember recording the show at the same time as having a party and trying to keep an eye on my parent's house!

This CD contains additional songs that were not broadcast, but it is not a complete show from that tour, as that would've required two discs. The only things missing are Hackett and Howe's lengthy solo segments that opened the show and 'Toe The Line': which was odd, as my radio recording has 'Toe The Line'.

The show is truly excellent. Bacon sings great here, and though he doesn't quite reach all the notes that he did in the studio, he's pretty on point. The Mover and Spalding rhythm section are seriously explosive, and the addition of keyboardist, Matt Clifford, (now a Rolling Stones sideman) was a *solid move, preferable to relying on the* guitar synthesizers.

The show opens with a ferocious version of 'Jekyll And Hyde', followed by an excellent 'Here I Wait'. A brand new song called 'Prizefighters' follows. It has some lovely hooks and the keyboards blend in well. Bacon really hits the higher end of his register here. An explosive version of 'Imagining' is followed by Hackett scorching his axe on 'Hackett To Bits', and the crowd eats it up. Throughout this recording, the audience excitement is palpable. There is no added crowd noise: these fans were really into the show.

After that, we get a gorgeous take on Hackett's 'Spectral Mornings', followed by the Genesis instrumental, '...In That Quiet Earth' (check out Mover's drumming on this one), which segues into the Genesis classic, 'I Know What I Like (In Your Wardrobe)'. They all sound really great and go down extremely well with the audience.

Then it's Howe's turn with the beautiful 'Sketches In The Sun' solo and a blistering version of his solo classic, 'Pennants'. Then it's time for the Yes classic, 'Roundabout', which is marvellous here: especially the performances from Bacon, Mover, Clifford and Spalding – the latter laying into the Chris Squire bass riffs with aplomb.

An incredible rendition of 'The Hunter' is the real show-stealer, and things conclude with 'You Can Still Get Through', 'Reach Out (Never Say No)', and of course 'When The Heart Rules The Mind', which is absolutely on fire here. It's great to have such an excellent recording of this snapshot in time as an official release.

PM Album
1:PM (1980)

Personnel:
Carl Palmer: drums, percussion
Erik Scott: bass, vocals
John Nitzinger: guitars, vocals

Barry Finnerty: guitars, vocals
Todd Cochran: keyboards, vocals
Released: 1980
Producer: PM

Well, what do you do if you are one of the world's greatest drummers, and you've been in Emerson, Lake & Palmer: one of the most successful rock bands of all time? It was 1979 when ELP broke up, and Carl Palmer decided to get with the times and form a band making new wave music. The band – PM – released their lone album *1:PM* in 1980 to an extremely disinterested public. Ariola Records issued the album in Europe only, which was rather odd, as it had a distinctively American sound. The idea was to do simplistic, catchy new wave songs with mass appeal. The end result was a weird mixed bag of bad and not so bad. One thing was clear: Carl wanted to lay back and let the songs take over. In fact, you'd be hard-pressed to believe this was even Palmer on drums. There's little evidence of his classic style, and few fills or patterns even stand out.

But the rest of the band had some chops. Nitzinger had a reputation in Texas as a good blues/rock guitar player and had recorded some solo albums; Finnerty had played with such jazz legends as Miles Davis and the Brecker Brothers; Scott had played with Alice Cooper and Flo & Eddie, and Cochran had been with Automatic Man.

The album's playing is loose but professional, though the production is decidedly average and the mix dry. Opening cut and lead single 'Dynamite' is a pop/rock song bordering on disco and is best forgotten. 'You've Got Me Rockin'' is as bad as its title. But songs like 'Dreamers' – with its call-and-response vocals – and the quirky 'Green Velvet Splendor', are actually quite fun, and you can hear traces of The Cars, Joe Jackson, Utopia, Blondie and The Knack in those songs.

'Go On, Carry On' is pretty lame boogie rock, but 'Do You Go All the Way' sounds like an amusing take on Devo and The Cars, with its zippy stop-start guitars and dancing keyboard fills.
This is definitely a guilty pleasure. 'Go For It' also goes for a hyper Devo-meets-Oingo-Boingo sound, and damn if it isn't fun yet awful at the same time.

Then there's 'Madeline': a slow-tempo song that sounds like an outtake from either Joe Jackson, The Hooters or Oingo Boingo, as there are nods to reggae and new wave, along with nice harmony guitars.

'You're Too Much' could've been on a John Hughes 1980s soundtrack like *Sixteen Candles*. It's another herky-jerky percolating new wave song. It has great synth work and nice choppy guitar power chords. 'Children Of The Air Age' is more a hard-rocking guitar cruncher, and with those tight guitar harmonies, is more fun than anything else.

As a whole, *1:PM* is an enjoyable, sprightly romp, that could've worked in the background at any 1980s party. It's a weird one, but if you approach it with an open mind, you will have some fun with it. Palmer may have had commerce in mind, but after all, the playing and singing are very good.

3 Albums
To The Power Of Three (1988)
Personnel:
Robert Berry: vocals, guitars and bass
Keith Emerson: keyboards
Carl Palmer: drums, percussion
Additional musicians: Suzie O'List, Kim Liatt Edwards, Lana Williams (backing vocals)
Released: 25 March 1988
Recorded: E-Zee Studios (London, UK) and West Side Studios (London, UK)
Producers: Robert Berry, Carl Palmer
Engineers: Steve McNeill, Ian Remmer, Peter Jones, Nick Davis
Illustration: The Cream Group
Highest Chart Position: US: 97

Formed in 1987, the band, 3, reunited Carl Palmer and Keith Emerson for the first time since the original ELP disbanded in 1979. From 1985-1987, Keith had been with the revamped ELP, as Emerson, Lake & Powell. Their 1986 album *Emerson, Lake & Powell* had done rather well, reaching the US Top 25 and UK Top 40 album charts, and had produced a hit with 'Touch And Go', which soared all the way to number 2 at Album Rock in the US, and number 60 on the singles charts. A tour followed that was rather good, but management, financial and personality issues put an end to this version of ELP.

In 1987, Palmer and Emerson met up with Robert Berry – who had briefly been in the proposed second version of GTR – and a deal was brokered with Geffen Records, which was rather ironic since Geffen had dumped Asia just the year before. John Kalodner – who had masterminded Asia's original formation – had his hand in this project as well, but the results were nowhere near the levels of success that Asia had, to say the least.

The music was pure AOR, with only a few nods to progressive rock and Emerson and Palmer fell prey to a lot of 1980s programming techniques and technology. The lead single 'Talkin' Bout' was a great one, though. Berry's voice was outstanding, the verses were nice and melodic, and the choruses dramatic and punchy. Berry here sounds like a cross between Yes's Trevor Rabin and Triumph's Gil Moore. The song's ending had a fantastic Berry vocal stretch, and Emerson added a nice piano fill in the fade-out. This was the album's best track. It climbed to number 9 on the US Album Rock charts, spending eleven weeks on the listings. You could not escape it on American radio that spring, but the video was given limited MTV rotation.

Much of the rest is radio-friendly pop with stiff keyboard and drum sounds typical of the times. Lyrics like 'Lover to Lover', 'Chains' and the abominable dance/rock cover of The Byrds classic, 'Eight Miles High' (with new and awful lyrics) are lowlights.

'Runaway' has some nice touches (though it sounds more like Bryan Adams or Loverboy), and 'You Do Or You Don't' is fair enough with some decent guitar-playing and singing. The marching 'On My Way Home' is a really lovely dedication to the late Tony Stratton-Smith – manager of The Nice, and founder of Charisma Records – who had passed away on 19 March 1987 was clearly on Emerson's mind. Marillion's 1987 masterpiece, *Clutching at Straws,* was also dedicated to the man known as 'Strat'.

'Desde La Vida' – the only true progressive rock song here – was a bold seven-minute tour de force featuring a variety of Emerson keyboard sequences, a classical piano solo, a Palmer drum solo, and impressive Berry guitar arpeggios on the up-tempo mid-section. The track could've been extended a bit more, but it's still pretty impressive.

The album struggled to number 97 in the US album charts, and the band – adding guitarist Paul Keller and two female backing singers – only toured clubs, playing a mix of songs from the album, a few ELP classics (though only instrumentals), and a cover of The Four Tops gem, 'Standing In The Shadows Of Love'. Emerson and Palmer had obligatory solos as well. A few shows were broadcast on FM radio and have seen semi-official release in so-so quality (my cassette copy of the Boston show is far better than what was released).

A major highlight for 3 was appearing at the Atlantic Records 40th Anniversary Concert on 14 May 1988 at Madison Square Garden in New York City. Other acts on the bill included Crosby, Stills & Nash, Genesis, Foreigner, The Bee Gees, The Spinners, Ben E. King, Yes, and a reformed Led Zeppelin, among many others. They were billed as Emerson and Palmer, due to the fact that Berry had no ties to Atlantic Records. They played 'America', which included parts of 'Rondo', 'Toccata' and 'Tank', with a Palmer drum solo.

3 became defunct in 1989, and plans for a sophomore album were scrapped. Emerson later stated that his heart wasn't really in it because the project was so commercial. Berry and Emerson began writing and did work together again in 2015 as 3.2. But Emerson's tragic death in 2016 ended that. In 2018, Berry finished the album, playing all instruments himself. Four of the songs were Emerson co-writes. It was issued as *The Rules Have Changed* and was a pretty impressive album, considering Berry had to piece things together in a few cases.

Berry received a positive response to this album and under the 3.2 moniker once again, he released his best album yet in 2020 titled *Third Impression* which contained excellent songs like 'Top of the World', 'A Fond Farewell' and a track co-written with Emerson before his passing called 'Never.' These last two albums as 3.2 show the talent that Berry has in a much better light than the first 3 album ever did.

Ride The Tiger albums
Ride The Tiger (2015)

Personnel:
Greg Lake: bass, acoustic and electric guitars, lead vocals
Geoff Downes; keyboards, programming
Michael Giles: drums, percussion
Released: 27 November 2015
Producers: Greg Lake, Geoff Downes
Recorded: 1989

In 1989, Greg Lake and Geoff Downes were without a band. Lake's last group had been Emerson, Lake & Powell, who disbanded in 1987, and Downes was last with Asia who disbanded in 1986. Although Geoff did record a solo album and produce GTR.

Lake and Downes had been together in Asia (briefly) back in late-1983/early-1984, where they enjoyed each other's company and talents, leading to this musical liaison. These demos were of a fairly good quality, though the drum programming is poor on some tracks. One needs to keep in mind, these were mostly sketches and not fully-formed songs yet. But label interest was slow to develop, leading to Downes reuniting with Asia in 1990 and Lake with the original ELP in 1991. The demos remained in the vaults.

However, some of the songs found a home rather soon. The gorgeous 'Love Under Fire' would be recorded by Asia as one of the best songs on 1992's *Aqua*, and the sublime 'Affairs Of The Heart' would also get recorded, this time by ELP for their 1992 *Black Moon* album. 'Street War' would be recorded by ELP for 1994's *In The Hot Seat*, while 'Money Talks' would be reworked into a much better form as 'Paper Blood' for ELP's *Black Moon*.

In late 2015, these demos finally saw release on Cherry Red Records. They were great to hear, even if some of the songs should've been best kept in the vaults. But they were clearly pretty polished demos and the sound quality is mostly good. Lake's former King Crimson bandmate, Michael Giles, supplied any real drums you hear.

'Love Under Fire' is very close to how Asia recorded it. It sounds attractive, with Lake's restrained vocals being perfect for the song. But 'Check it Out' is painful dance/rock that never went further than this collection, thankfully. 'Money Talks' is also pretty poor, ending up a far better song with ELP, as 'Paper Blood', mentioned above. 'Blue Light' is a so-so pop tune with some usable sections and some that needed to be discarded.

'Affairs Of The Heart' is a rough demo with clattering programming and is one of many tracks here where Downes uses obnoxious-sounding trumpet synth patches. But the melodies are beautiful, as are all of the lyrics. The ELP version was far superior, with an added bridge. An acoustic-based recording by ELP, it scored limited airplay in the US in 1992 and almost always appears on ELP compilations.

'Street War' is far removed from the synth-punk of the 1994 ELP version, but you can hear the potential from the slower and more moody demo. The music is almost completely different, but Downes does a solo that sounds like Keith Emerson to a degree. Also included is an alternate mix of 'Love Under Fire', with different drums and a slightly altered arrangement.

I, like many fans, always wanted to hear these demos, and while there's not much intriguing or revolutionary here, it's still to have this release.

Greg was still alive when these demos were issued and said the following in a press release on the Cherry Red Records website:

To be honest, I thought that these recordings had simply disappeared off the radar screen until one of my management team, Daniel Earnshaw, reminded me of their existence. My initial reaction was not entirely positive, as I generally view many of these re-releases to be a bit tiresome. However, upon hearing these recordings again, I immediately identified their value, both in terms of songwriting and of musicianship and production. Geoff, of course, is a masterful musician, with an instinctive ability to maximize the potential of any song, both as a player and as an arranger. His contribution to these recordings is clear for all to see, and for me, it was a real pleasure to reflect upon our friendship together, both personally and as musicians.

Downes also gave a statement on this release on the label's website promoting the album:

One of the privileges in my career has been the opportunity to embrace a number of bespoke projects with some of the world's greatest musicians. Greg Lake, of course, was at the forefront of the progressive revolution, the lead vocalist and bassist with both King Crimson and ELP: bands which literally changed the world, pushing boundaries of excellence and creativity, creating a brand new musical genre from London, which would soon captivate the planet. This collection of songs represents a particularly creative period in my life. I'm delighted that Greg and I have rekindled our friendship and worked together again to share this collection with you.

Solo Albums

John Wetton Solo Studio albums
Caught in the Crossfire (1980)
Wetton/Manzanera (1987) w/Phil Manzanera
Voice Mail (also known as *Battle Lines*) (1994)
Arkangel (1997)
Sinister (also known as *Welcome to Heaven*) (2000)
Rock of Faith (2003)
Raised in Captivity (2011)

Geoff Downes Solo Studio Albums
The Light Program (1987)
Vox Humana (1992)
Evolution (1996)
The World Service (2000)
Shadows & Reflections (2003)
Electronica (2010)
Pictures of You (2012) w/Chris Braide
Suburban Ghosts (2015) w/Chris Braide
Skyscraper Souls (2017) w/Chris Braide
Halcyon Hymns (2021) w/Chris Braide

Steve Howe Solo Studio Albums
Beginnings (1975)
The Steve Howe Album (1979)
Turbulence (1991)
The Grand Scheme of Things (1993)
Masterpiece Guitars (1996) w/Martin Taylor
Quantum Guitar (1998)
Portraits of Bob Dylan (1999)
Natural Timbre (2001)
The 3 Ages of Magick (2001) w/Oliver Wakeman
Skyline (2002)
Elements (2003)
Spectrum (2005)
Motif (2008)
The Haunted Melody (2008) w/Steve Howe Trio
Travelling (2010) w/Steve Howe Trio
Time (2011)
Nexus (2017) w/Virgil Howe
New Frontier (2019) w/Steve Howe Trio
Love Is (2020)

Carl Palmer Solo Albums
Live in the Hood (2000) as part of Qango
Working Live, Volume 1 (2002) w/Carl Palmer Band
Working Live, Volume 2 (2004) w/Carl Palmer Band
Working Live, Volume 3 (2010) w/Carl Palmer Band
Live in the USA (2016) w/Carl Palmer's ELP Legacy
Live (2018) w/Carl Palmer's ELP Legacy

John Payne Solo Albums
Windows to the Soul (2006) as part of GPS
Military Man (2009) EP as Asia featuring John Payne
Recollections (2014) as Asia featuring John Payne
Dukes of the Orient (2018) as part of Dukes of the Orient
Freakshow (2020) as part of Dukes of the Orient

References And Bibliography

Although much of this book came from my own knowledge and interviews, there were some great interviews and websites that I was more than pleased to utilise. The websites were as follows:

johnwettonlegacy.co.uk
geoffdownes.com
originalasia.com
vintagerock.com
classicrockrevisited.com

And the books I used for some quotes and references (including my own book) were as follows:

Braidis, P. *Unstrung Heroes: Fifty Guitar Players You Should Know (*Schiffer Publishing, 2016)
Gallant, D. *Asia: The Heat Goes On, The Authorized Asia Biography* (David Gallant Publishing, 2004)
Whitburn, J. *Rock Tracks 1981-2008* (Record Research Inc., 2008)

I also personally conducted interviews with Rik Emmett, Steve Hackett, Steve Howe and David Kilminster. Some of this interview material comes from my book, though not all of it that appears here was in that published work.

I highly suggest reading David Gallant's book, which had its first edition in 2001, and an updated version in 2004. A new book called *Asia-Heat of the Moment* came out around the time of the reunion in 2007 and is more or less a re-write of the previous books, with updated information on the reunion and a scaling back of the info on the Payne era.

Would you like to write for Sonicbond Publishing?

We are mainly a music publisher, but we also occasionally publish in other genres including film and television. At Sonicbond Publishing we are always on the look-out for authors, particularly for our two main series, On Track and Decades.

Mixing fact with in depth analysis, the On Track series examines the entire recorded work of a particular musical artist or group. All genres are considered from easy listening and jazz to 60s soul to 90s pop, via rock and metal.

The Decades series singles out a particular decade in an artist or group's history and focuses on that decade in more detail than may be allowed in the On Track series.

While professional writing experience would, of course, be an advantage, the most important qualification is to have real enthusiasm and knowledge of your subject. First-time authors are welcomed, but the ability to write well in English is essential.

Sonicbond Publishing has distribution throughout Europe and North America, and all our books are also published in E-book form. Authors will be paid a royalty based on sales of their book. Further details about our books are available from www.sonicbondpublishing.com. To contact us, complete the contact form there or email info@sonicbondpublishing.co.uk